RHINO PRESENTS

FORGOTTEN FADS and FABULOUS FLOPS

BY PAUL KIRCHNER

AN AMAZING COLLECTION OF GOOFY STUFF THAT SEEMED LIKE A GOOD IDEA AT THE TIME

GPG

GENERAL PUBLISHING GROUP

Los Angeles

Publisher: W. Quay Hays
Editor: Harold Bronson
Managing Editor: Colby Allerton
Production Director: Nadeen Torio
Production Assistants: Catherine Vo Bailey, Gaston Moraga
Copy Editor: Peter Hoffman

Special thanks to Julie D'Angelo, Phil Dupuoy and Sheryl Winter

For information:
General Publishing Group, Inc.
2701 Ocean Park Boulevard, Suite 140
Santa Monica, CA 90405

Library of Congress Cataloging-in-Publication Data

Kirchner, Paul.
    Forgotten fads and fabulous flops : an amazing collection of goofy
stuff that seemed like a good idea at the time / by Paul Kirchner.
        p.   cm.
    Includes bibliographical references and index.
    ISBN 1-881649-44-X
    1. Fads--United States--History--20th century. 2. Popular
culture--United States--History--20th century. 3. Americana.
    I. Title.
    E169.02.K555   1995
    306.4'0973--dc20
                                                                    95-7742
                                                                    CIP

Printed in the USA
10 9 8 7 6 5 4 3 2 1

General Publishing Group
Los Angeles

CONTENTS

INTRODUCTION

Nobody sets out to fail. Everything in this book started out as a dream of success. No matter how stupid that dream may seem in retrospect, it was strong enough to bring something new into the world. For that, the dreamers deserve respect. They tried, and in so doing, made the world a little more interesting. Every stab at success carries with it the possibility of failure, and wherever there's creativity, there's going to be as many bad ideas generated as good. But each idea good or bad represents a new choice, and contributes to a sense of life's infinite possibilities. I'm glad I live in a world that offers me flying cars and insect food, even if I do not choose to partake. I'm also reassured that the responsible adults aren't nipping every foolish endeavor in the bud, that there's still room for the half-baked and the harebrained.

This book does not pretend to be a complete encyclopedia of the failed and the forgotten. I have tried to present a variety of the familiar and the obscure, significant and inconsequential, from as many different facets of human endeavor as I could find, delivering a variety of cautionary tales. Some cost great corporations hundreds of millions of dollars, others the lifetime of a true believer. Several were the pet projects of people who accomplished great things in other areas. Even if they retreated from the marketplace under a fusillade of overripe fruit, their stories deserve to be told. Some might ask why, in a society that worships success, we should devote any attention to things that have failed. It can be instructive, of course, but more than that, it's therapeutic. A sojourn into the world of flops restores the equilibrium. It establishes most of us at our rightful place in the happy medium. We may not enjoy astonishing success, but at the same time, we have not carved our likenesses onto the Mt. Rushmore of stupefying failure. We can't all be Henry Ford, but let's be grateful that we have not devoted our lives to the design of an iceberg aircraft carrier. For every Miller Lite there's a Hop'n Gator. For every *E.T.* there's an *Inchon*.

We're entitled to a laugh at their expense, but let's not be too harsh. Most of these ideas had a lot of love invested in them. As Harold Frankel, a toy industry executive, reminded me, "Every child is beautiful. At least to its parents."

To Tom Conroy,
Sage, Seer, Soothsayer,
and Photo Archivist Extraordinaire;
and to my wife Sandy,
and the kids Emily, Eric and Toni,
for their ongoing indulgence.

ACKNOWLEDGMENTS

Among the people who contributed to this effort were Ian Tetrault, computer services; the staff of the Hamden Town Library; Movie Still Archives of Harrison, Nebraska; Colin Randall of *Bookseller*, London; Harold Frankel of Laramie Toys; Adam Philips, of DC Comics; William Baron of LCI, Inc.; George Miller, beer can collector; American Beer Institute; Kathie Jones of Urinette; Bob McCoy of the Museum of Questionable Medical Devices; Robert McMath of the New Products Showcase and Learning Center; Trina Robbins, Scott Buttfield, Hans Riemer, Ernie Stiner, Chris Ruel, Bob Jackson, Steve Iacoviello, Bhob Stewart, Harold and Kiki Rabinowitz, and Larry Hama.

Readers with amusing examples of flops, blunders, and misconceived notions are invited to send them to the author through the General Publishing Group, 2701 Ocean Park Blvd., Suite 140, Santa Monica, CA 90405. Verifiable contributions will be acknowledged and may be included in future compilations, with atrribution.

AMPHICAR

Okay, let's get it over with—if Teddy Kennedy had had one of these he might have been President.

In the late 1950s Hanns Trippel, who had designed amphibious vehicles for the German military, applied his expertise to the civilian market and came up with the Amphicar. It was a sporty-looking convertible with two propellers tucked under the rear bumper and an undercut front-end for that seaworthy appearance. The front wheels functioned as rudders (sort of) when the car was afloat. With its 38 hp Triumph 4-cylinder engine it promised 72 mph on land and 5 mph in the water.

Some 2500 Amphicars were produced between 1961 and 1967, many of them imported into the United States. It should have owned a piece of the market. This was the heyday of the James Bond craze, and a car that would enable its driver to escape pursuers at any convenient body of water would seem just the thing for aspiring 007s. Nevertheless, few were sold. Perhaps it was the fact that at $3395 the Amphicar was as expensive as a Chevy Biscayne *plus* a boat and trailer. Perhaps it was the Amphicar's anemic performance on either land or sea; as *Car and Driver* put it, "They took the worst features of a car and the worst features of a boat and combined them..." Probably it was its unfortunate tendency to rust out once it had been immersed a few times.

The idea has not been totally retired. The French Hobbycar and the German Amphi-Ranger both attempted to resuscitate interest in amphibious passenger cars, but neither made much of a splash. In 1994, *Popular Mechanics* reported on the Aquastrada Delta, a souped-up amphicar developed by a group of Northern California entrepreneurs. Its body is fiberglass, styled like a Corvette, and its wheels retract into the hull for nautical use. Its 245-hp Ford engine delivers 100-mph on land, and with its jet pump propulsion, 45-mph at sea. The Delta would sell for between $25,000 and $35,000.

The Amphicar was far from the worst amphibious vehicle on record. The United States Army once spent $200 million for 1400 "Gamma Goat" amphibious trucks that were incapable of floating. Their performance on land was bad enough—they frequently broke down—and in water they generally sank like stones.

ANIMAL OF THE MONTH CLUB

Creative Playthings, known for Scandinavian-style educational toys and natural wood swingsets, was the original politically correct toy company. Inspired by the popularity of book-of-the-month clubs for adults, Creative Playthings introduced the "Animal of the Month Club" for kids in 1968. Children who subscribed would receive an exotic "pet" delivered through the mail each month, such as an Argentine toad, snails, musk turtles, newts, Mongolian gerbils, and more. It was hard enough scouring the Argentinian swamps to fill four thousand orders for toads, but an even bigger problem arose. Many of the pets sent out to eager subscribers arrived dead, squashed, or dehydrated. Envy the lucky parent explaining that to a six-year-old! Rather than change the name of its line to "Dead Animal of the Month Club," Creative Playthings chose to discontinue the line.

ANTISEASICK STEAMER

Sir Henry Bessemer was a British inventor and engineer who is best known for his 1856 process for manufacturing mild steel. That and his many other successful patents earned him considerable wealth, as well as a knighthood. Business required him to travel to the Continent regularly, a voyage he dreaded due to his chronic seasickness. The nineteenth-century inventor did not passively accept such indignities, though, and Bessemer soon came up with a solution. He designed a steamship with a cylindrical cavity running bow-to-stern above its keel. Inside this housing, the ship's large public lounge, called the "saloon," balanced on a teeter-totter intended to keep it level no matter how the ship rolled. He drew up plans with the help of R.J. Reed, a naval architect, and in 1874 launched the cross-channel steamer he christened the *Bessemer*.

In actual practice the "swinging saloon' did not work as Bessemer had intended. Its pivoting action actually

caused it to roll more violently than the fixed deck above
it. The inventor tried to rectify the situation by installing
hydraulic pistons to control the movement of the saloon,
but this induced more nausea than the pivot. Giving up,
Sir Henry had the saloon locked into position so that the
Bessemer could be used as a conventional steamer. Its
unusual design made it difficult to steer though, and on
its first trip it collided with the piers in both Dover and
Callais. Sir Henry sold his ship for scrap, but that did not
end its troubles. The saloon, which had found a home at
an English horticultural college, was hit by a German
bomb in World War II and blown to pieces.

AROMARAMA,
SMELL-O-VISION AND ODORAMA

"You must breathe it to believe it!" read the come-on for *Behind the Great Wall*. Released in 1959, it was the first movie that attempted to captivate its audience by their nostrils. Public relations man Charles Weiss added a 'scent track' to Italian film maker Count Leonardo Bonzi's travelogue of Red China, and dubbed the effect AromaRama. It transmitted signals to a special device which could emit 31 different scents—including bread, coffee, oil paint, gun smoke, incense and peppermint—keyed to appropriate scenes. The scents were dispersed throughout the theater by the air-conditioning system, carried on a quickly-evaporating base of freon. A

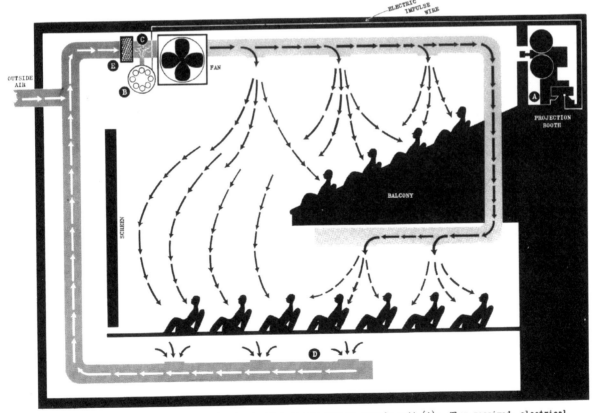

THE AROMARAMA SYSTEM...Film has extra track which issues cues to console unit (A). When received, electrical impulse is sent to turntable (B). Proper odor can is rotated and discharged into air stream (C). Odor is disseminated simultaneously throughout entire auditorium and is then removed through intake ducts (D) to pass through electronic air purifier (E). Air in theatre now cleansed for new odor to be discharged on cue.

subsequent cue signaled the air-conditioner to suck out the scent through a special filter to remove the odor. It was claimed that all members of the audience would get the smell within two seconds, and that the odor could be withdrawn from the theater just as quickly. The idea is intriguing— after all, there is something about an odor which can trigger long-forgotten memories and associations. However, the system did not work out as well as Weiss had hoped. One problem was with the quality of the chemical scents. The smell of a beautiful grove of pine in Peking was reminiscent of a sub-way restroom on disinfectant day. Another problem was the difficulty of delivering to every member of the audience the right intensity of scent at the right time. Those sitting clos-est to the air-conditioning system got overpowering blasts, while those farthest away got very little. Also, the air condi-tioning had trouble removing all traces of scent, so that while crossing the Gobi Desert the smell of rain-drenched spring grass might still fill the air.

"First they moved (1895)! Then they talked (1927)! Now they smell!" read the poster for Mike Todd Jr.'s *Scent of Mystery* (1960). It employed Smell-O-Vision, an improve-ment over AromaRama in that each seat had its own tube piping scents directly to the occupant's nose. This contrivance was accorded the fanfare of a major scientific breakthrough, with advance publicity claiming that "Osmologist" Hans Laube had carefully selected each "olfaction" from his "library of essences" to ensure authen-ticity. This was supposed to justify the inflated ticket price of $3.50. A mystery that took its audience gallivanting across Spain, the film used smells as clues: the Chiappelli perfume of the "mystery woman," and the pipe tobacco aroma of the villain. Other olfactory delectations included apples, peaches, brandy, shoe polish, roses and garlic. Customers came, sniffed, and left unimpressed. Critics described it as the first movie that stunk on purpose.

The AromaRama and Smell-O-Vision processes were expensive to install, difficult to maintain, and unreliable at the best of times. And neither attracted much of an audience. However, a theater owner's profit is generated

IN *SCENT OF MYSTERY* THE AUDIENCE NOT ONLY SAW THE DONKEY, BUT SMELLED IT.

at the refreshment stand, and some of those who had invested in the scent-dispersal equipment suggested that it might pay off if they used it to deliver the smell of buttered popcorn to their patrons.

The most recent attempt to add the weapon of smell to the moviemaker's arsenal was in 1981, when bad-taste maven John Waters released *Polyester* in "Odorama." Audiences were given scratch 'n' sniff cards, and cued by numbers on the screen to scratch the appropriate scent at the appropriate time. Odors ranged from roses to dirty sneakers; that that's as far as it went should come as a relief to anyone familiar with Waters' *Pink Flamingos*.

BALLBUSTER

From a grid-like frame sprouted a number of wire stalks each topped with a hinged red plastic ball. The 1976 Mego Toy Company catalog describes the action: "Use your balls to bust your opponents, if you can. Break 'em all and you're a winner, too! A family game that's loads of fun. Swing your balls on their flexible rods and pop your opponents' tops."

What to call this game of skill for the whole family? What else but "Ballbuster"? Many strange things have happened in this world of ours, but few stranger than the fact that through product development, package design, focus groups and the development of the ad campaign, this name survived.

When Mego presented its line to buyers from all the major toy and department store chains, the Ballbuster

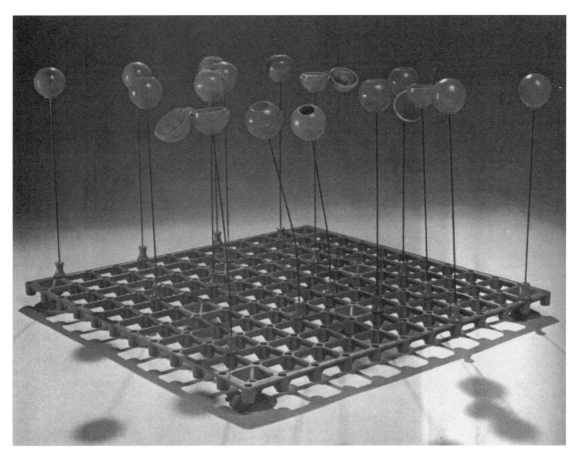

television commercial was shown to the assemblage. The requisite nuclear family enjoyed some quality time with the game, after which the children scampered off and the husband turned to his wife, smiling, and said, "Honey, you're a *real* ballbuster!"

The stunned silence that followed triggered the first suspicions that Ballbuster was not destined to displace Parcheesi on the pantheon of classic games.

BANANA SKIN HIGH

"Electrical banana is gonna be a sudden craze,
  Electrical banana is bound to be the very next phase."
Donovan protested innocence, but his hit song *Mellow Yellow* gave credence to rumors in 1967 that there was psychedelic potential in the cheap and legal banana peel. The *Berkeley Barb* reported that a friend of the drummer for Country Joe and the Fish had discovered hitherto-unknown potential in the popular fruit. The peels had to be prepared, of course. The *Barb* advised readers to scrape out the white fiber from the inside of the banana peel, boil it into a paste and dry it in an oven at 200 degrees, then smoke the resulting residue in a pipe or joint. New York's *East Village Other* and *The Los Angeles Free Press* reprinted the recipe, and grocery stores experienced a run on the fruit.

At Central Park's 1967 "Be-in," hippies chanted "banana, banana." One carried an over-sized wooden banana totem. Some wore t-shirts emblazoned with the logo of the United Fruit Co. An entreprenuer in Haight-Ashbury began selling the banana peel preparation at $5 per half-ounce; the bananas themselves he gave away for free. The *Mellow Yellow Cookbook* soon appeared with recipes incorporating banana peels.

Some hippies claimed that banana peels produced "a gentle high." One said "Your limbs feel light." Others admitted to getting little out of the experience besides an intimate acquaintance with the taste of burnt compost. There was nothing new in that, of course: among the substances smoked in the sixties were catnip, chlorine-soaked lettuce, green peppers allowed to rot and then dried, and (reportedly) spider webs. *Time* and *Newsweek* retained their skepticism, while mentioning that banana skins do contain serotonin, a neurochemical related to mind-benders psilocybin and dimethyl tryptamine. A spokesman for the United Fruit Company insisted that "The only trip you can take with a banana is when you slip on the peel."

The original story in the *Berkeley Barb* had been a hoax. As it went out on the grapevine, the joke was lost. If anyone ever got high on the drug it was pure testimony to the power of positive thinking.

BEATLE IMITATORS

In the Beatlemaniacal mid-1960s, a number of rock bands sought to emulate the Fab Four as closely as possible. If their talent was hard to match, their name and appearance were not nearly so. Some of the bands seeking to confuse the record buyer were:

- *Beatle Mania!* by The Liverpools, described as "Four *liver*-uppers who have *pooled* their talents."
- *Do the Beetle* by Brock and the Sultans, contains such hits as Beetle Walk, 30 Lb. Beetle, Feed the Beetle, Fast Beetle, Mexican Beetle and Little Brown Beetle.
- *Beat-A-Mania*, no artists credited.
- *Beats!!!!* by The Merseyside Sound! The New Beat from Britain!!!!!
- *The Beatle Buddies*, an album by a girl group of the same name. They advertised their "fabulous BEATLE sound" and sang their own version of Beatle hits including "He Loves You" and "I Wanna Hold Your Hand," as well as their own compositions. The album cover shows them glumly posed (with bangs, of course) to resemble their buddies on "Meet the Beatles," and liner notes promised that this "cute and talented" foursome had "looks and sound destined to last long after the Beatles are gone."
- *The Beetle Beat*, by the Buggs, featuring actual Beatle hits as well as original compositions including "Teddy

Boy Stomp."

- *Beatlerama*, headlined as "The Fabulous New Sound From England," sung by The Manchesters.
- *Beattle Mash* by The Liverpool Boys, who appear from their photos to have left boyhood far behind.
- *Best of the Beatles* was put out by Pete Best, who was replaced by Ringo just prior to the Beatles' spectacular success. He later put together another group and thus was able to justify the play on words in its title. If anyone was ever entitled to sneak a piece of the Beatles' pie, surely it was Best.
- *All About the Beatles* was put out by Louise Harrison Caldwell, George Harrison's sister.

BEERS THAT WENT FLAT

Gablinger's—Several low-cal beers were marketed in the sixties, and all of them flailed. The biggest flop of them all was Rheingold's 1967 entry, Gablinger's, sometimes called the "Edsel of Beers." Its can featured the visage of its formulator, Swiss chemist Hersch Gablinger, who looks exactly like you would expect a Swiss chemist to look. Rheingold claimed that Gablinger's was brewed with the same ingredients as a normal beer, but it included a mysterious carbohydrate-destroying enzyme. "It doesn't fill you up" read its label, and its ads showed a slice of bread in a mug to illustrate the carbohydrate content of other beers. Despite a saturation ad campaign, it didn't sell. Marketers claim that beer-drinkers, many of whom regard their bellies as a "work in progress," won't respond to a campaign based on weight control. The subsequent, successful light beers made sure that their "less filling" message implied that you could drink more, not shed the gut. Then again, perhaps beer drinkers just didn't go for a beer that was watery, tasted lousy and wouldn't hold a head.

Hop'n Gator beer was put on the market by the Pittsburgh Brewing Company in 1969. Developed by Dr. Robert Cade, the inventor of Gatorade, it was a mixture of beer and Gatorade, with approximately 25% more alcohol content than your standard brew. Ketchum, McLeod & Grove, the ad agency responsible for promoting the concoction, adopted a "fun" approach to the campaign, with the theme, "You may forget the name, but you'll never forget the taste," which was hard to argue with. It's true that jocks drink a lot of Gatorade and sports fans drink a lot of beer, but this combination violates God's law.

Fruit-Flavored Beers—Between 1969 and 1971, several breweries produced "alcoholic soda pops" that were the beer equivalent of the successful wine coolers. There was Hamm's Right Time Red, with a sweet, cherry flavor for females who wanted to get fruit looped, and Right Time Gold, with a tart, grapefruit taste for the guys. In 1970, National Brewing of St. Paul marketed Malt Duck, a beer and grape juice blend. In the same year Lone Star marketed Lime Lager. Said a company executive, "It's caught on with an unusual beer drinker—one who doesn't like the taste of beer but likes lime." Unfortunately, that beer drinker was so unusual that very little Lime Lager was sold.

I had this beer brewed up just for me. I think it's the best I ever tasted. And I've tasted a lot. I think you'll like it, too.

Billy Beer—Billy Carter holds the "Most Embarrassing First Brother" title in perpetuity. He kept the press busy with his redneck musings and Libyan business deals, and even got in trouble for urinating on a wall at the Atlanta airport. Yet he still found time to devote to his own special cause: beer. Not just drinking it, not just illegally selling it on Sundays out of his gas station, not just voiding it onto airport walls, but promoting his own brand. "Billy" beer was first marketed in 1977 by the Falls City Brewing Company of Louisville, Kentucky, and then licensed to several other breweries. At the top of the label it proudly proclaimed: "Brewed expressly for and with the personal approval of one of America's Great Beer Drinkers—Billy Carter." At the bottom a message read: "I had this beer brewed up just for me. I think it's the best I ever tasted. And I've tasted a lot. I think you'll like it, too." Underneath that was the First Brother's signature. Those who sampled "Billy" said it tasted as if it had already passed through the man himself. It profited from the 1970s beer can collecting craze, as every collector put aside a few six-packs confident that it would soon disappear and that cans of it would prove to be a good investment. After Billy Carter declared his alcoholism and went into rehab in 1978, his beer went belly up. Even now, though, "Billy" cans are so common that they've been handed out for free at can collectors' conventions as a publicity stunt. Still, the dream lives on, fueled by coups such as that of Johnnie Parsons of West Virginia. He put an ad in a Washington, D.C., newspaper, and sold a full case of "Billy" for $2,000.

Nude Beer—In the mid-eighties, Golden Beverages of Irvine, California, marketed Nude Beer. Its bottle featured photos of women whose bikini tops could be scratched off by those who might be curious as to what was under them. What was under them was indeed impressive. The beer didn't receive much attention until police in Colorado branded it obscene and took it off store shelves, temporarily boosting sales. In 1986, the National Organization of Women perked up sales again with a petition and letter-writing campaign against the product. A spokeswoman for the company argued that "The labels aren't real suggestive. It's more like a portrait...And then again, you don't *have* to scratch the top off." You don't *have* to, but after your third or fourth beer your resistance drops. The company announced plans to sponsor Miss Nude Beer contests at bars. Entrants would be given Nude Beer

T-shirts which they could cut into whatever shape they wanted; the best design would win. Contestants wouldn't be required to wear bottoms, but the company expressed its hope that they would. "We don't want this to be sleazy or anything," said marketing director Fred Jacobson. The company also produced Nude Nuts and planned to come out with Nude Cigarettes.

Harley-Davidson Heavy Beer—Well, the kind of guys that wear greasy black t-shirts over hairy beer bellies don't drink *light* beer, do they? A welcome flash of rebellion against creeping wimpiness, but unfortunately this full-bodied brew from 1988 did not catch on.

Dry Beer—In 1990, three of America's premier brewers fell in love with the idea of dry beer, which was supposed to offer a "cleaner finish," whatever that means. Despite $40 million in advertising for the category, Coors Dry, Bud Dry, and Michelob Dry were not able to grab even 2% of the market. As marketing consultant Jack Trout put it, "Nobody can figure out what the hell dry beer is. The opposite of wet beer?" As of now, dry beer still hangs on, though barely.

BELLY BONGO

In the 1970s, a perplexing television commercial appeared. It featured a multi-cultural mob, young and old, all of whom wore a colored plastic square on their abdomens, to which was attached a rubber ball on a string. All were doing a twist-like dance movement—not to dislodge the ungainly device, but to make the ball bounce back and forth against it. A bouncy lyric explained the activity:

"Get a Belly Bongo, strap it on tight, turn up the music—all right!

Now shake it! Make it! Do your thing like mad!

27

Liven up the party—Belly Bongo's super bad!"

This, and the grin afixed to everyone in the crowd made it clear—these people were having fun! They were representative of the millions of Americans soon to be swept up in this latest craze! The millions of Americans who would soon buy millions of Belly Bongos for themselves!

So go the happy dreams of failed fadmongers everywhere.

BOOKS OF LIMITED APPEAL

Even in the publishing business, books are judged by their covers. Starting in the 1970s, the Diagram Group has enlivened the staid proceedings of the Frankfurt Book Fair with a contest: a magnum of champagne goes to the person who submits the most improbable title on offer. The results are published annually in the *Bookseller*, a London journal of the publishing trade. The winners were:

1978 *Proceedings of the Second International Workshop on Nude Mice* (University of Tokyo Press)

1979 *The Madam as Entrepreneur: Career Management in House Prostitution* (Transaction Press)

1980 *The Joy of Chickens* (Prentice Hall), described as "a history and celebration of the chicken."

1981 *Last Chances at Love—Terminal Romances* (Pinnacle Books)

1982 Award was split between *Braces Owners' Manual: A Guide to the Wearing and Care of Braces* (Patient Information Library) and *Population and Other Problems* (China National Publications). It's hard to understand how either beat that year's *Tourists' Guide to Lebanon.*

1983 *The Theory of Lengthwise Rolling* (MIR—a Soviet publishing house)

1984 *The Book of Marmalade: Its Antecedents, Its History and Its Role in the World Today*

1985 *Natural Breast Enlargement with Total Mind Power: How to Use the Other 90 Percent of Your Mind to Increase the Size of Your Breasts*

(Westwood Publishing Co.)

1986 *Oral Sadism and the Vegetarian Personality*
(Brunner/Mazel), beating out non-vegetarian entries
The Aerodynamics of Pork (Sphere), and
Cannibalism and the Common Law (University of
Chicago Press). There was no prize given in 1987.

1988 *Versailles—The View From Sweden* (University of
Chicago Press)

1989 *How to Shit in the Woods: An Environmentally
Sound Approach to a Lost Art* (Ten Speed Press),
won the prize only after careful consideration. The
judges would not have considered it if it were
found to be intentionally humorous. The catalogue
blurb helped:

"Most of the outdoor books available in English
fall prey to Victorian sensibilities, failing to mention
one of the most serious issues encountered in
trekking around the countryside. The author, a long-
time river-runner and outdoors person, introduces
genteel folks to one of the fundamental realities of
life in the woods."

1990 *Lesbian Sadomasochism Safety Manual* (Lace
Publications). No prize for 1991.

1992 *How to Avoid Huge Ships* (Cornell Maritime Press)
won hands down, and kudos for addressing a serious
matter that receives less than its share of attention.

1993 *American Bottom Archaeology* (University of
Illinois Press)

1994 *Highlights in the History of Concrete* (British
Cement Association)

Among the finalists over the years are some that
should be at least temporarily rescued from oblivion. Feel-
good titles include:

Macramé Gnomes
Biochemist Songbook
*Nasal Maintenance: Nursing Your Nose through
Troubled Times*
Living with Antiques in New Zealand

Big and Very Big Hole Drilling (Technical Publishing
House, Bucharest)

Sodomy and the Pirate Tradition (New York
University Press)

Why Replace a Missing Back Tooth (Quintessence
Publishing of Kingston on Thames)

*An Introduction to the Biology of British Littoral
Barnacles* (Field Studies Council)

Inflammatory Bowel Diseases: A Personal View
(Yearbook Medical Publishers)

Detecting Fake Nazi Regalia

*The Potatoes of Bolivia: Their Breeding, Value, and
Evolutionary Relationships* (Oxford University Press)

How to Write While You Sleep (North Light Books)

The Social History of Gas Masks (Wordwright Books)

The New Websters Encyclopaedia of Dictionaries
(Ottenheimer Publishers) We're actually looking for
a dictionary of encyclopedias, but thanks anyway.

The Teach Your Chicken to Fly Training Manual
(Houghton Mifflin Australia)

Why Do We Pursue the Holohedron? (MITA Press)

*Benedictine Maledictions: Liturgical Cursing in
Romanesque France* (Cornell University Press)

101 Super Uses for Tampon Applicators (PBS)

Psychiatric Disorders in Dental Practice (John Wright)

BOSOM MAKEUP, ETC.

What with see-through blouses, topless swimsuits,
Woodstock and other unconstrained social events, the
breast had to look its best in the 1960s. In 1969, New York
hairdresser and designer Kenneth put out a line of bosom
makeup, including brushes, creams and rouge. It included
a "cleavage delineator" and a "tip blush," which was
"drawn across tips in a circular motion to achieve a glis-
tening rosy hue."

Fashion trends in the sixties opened the market for
other odd innovations in cosmetics. Miniskirts created a

problem that wouldn't be solved until the invention of pantyhose—how to keep from revealing that unsightly band at the top of nylon stockings, not to mention the garters that held them up? Tights were one choice. Then Givenchy offered leg makeup to cover the lengthy expanse revealed by miniskirts. It came in shocking pink, violet mauve, turquoise blue, and sea green. There was also Knee Glo, a powder rouge for knees. And vinyl winking-eye appliqués to go on the knees as decoration.

Coty sold Body Paint, in lime, blue and mauve as well as flesh tone, allowing the miniskirt-wearer to coordinate her skin color with her outfit. As the ad read: "No body who loves mini, kicky, bare-as-you-dare fashions looks dressed without it. (Coty Originals gives you a *face* for every fashion, and now a *body* too.)"

It came in a small paint can and included a miniature paint roller and tray, all for $6.

BRANDO: SONGS MY MOTHER TAUGHT ME

The publishing industry is secretive about its failures, so it's hard to nail down a definitive flop except by rumor and deduction. Ronald Reagan's autobiography, for which he reputedly received a $7 million dollar advance, had a notably brief tenure on the best-seller list. The book was sanitized and self-serving, but what else would anyone expect? Quite unsanitized and not particularly self-serving was the autobiographical *Brando: Songs My Mother Taught Me*. Brando, who has in recent years made a career of being overpaid for his efforts, is supposed to have received close to $6 million as his advance. He began work in 1991, but after making little headway on his own got the assistance of Robert Lindsey, who had also ghost-written, coincidentally, the Reagan autobiography. When the book was released in September, 1994, Brando refused to give any interviews for it outside of a peculiar 90-minute special with Larry King, whom he called "darling" and kissed on the lips.

The 458-page opus received mixed reviews. *Entertainment Weekly's* critic called it an "agglomeration of free-associative cud-chewing that seems lardy and bloated... a rambling belch..." Most critics were unmoved by Brando's discussion of his occasional bulimia and childhood love of farting contests. In a special sidebar, *Time* magazine noted his fixation with oral hygiene: he discusses the breath odor of his mother and his governess; speculates on the bacterial content of a paparazzo's mouth; and claims to have found his onstage kisses with Tallulah Bankhead so repulsive that he followed each one up with a swig of mouthwash.

The book made a brief cameo apearance on the bestseller list of *The New York Times Book Review*, peaking at number eight one week and dangling from the bottom rung for another three, in a year that saw smashing literary successes from lesser theatrical lights Tim Allen (of *Home Improvement*) and Paul Reiser (of *Mad About You*).

BREAKFAST CEREAL WITH FREEZE-DRIED FRUIT

Many people like to put fruit on their cornflakes, so packaging cereal with the fruit already included seems an obvious marketing ploy. In 1964, Post thought it had arrived at a way to do this. NASA had developed the freeze-drying process, whereby food is quick-frozen and then placed in a high vacuum to remove all its moisture. When liquid is added, the food is reconstituted. Post added freeze-dried strawberries to its cornflakes. The product was a surprise hit, and Post prepared to meet the demand. It introduced freeze-dried blueberries and peaches, and built a new multi-million dollar facility to produce "Fruit in the Box Cereal." Kellogg's followed suit with "Corn Flakes with Instant Bananas." Kellogg's planned a major promotional campaign, with Jimmy Durante singing "Yes, We Have No Bananas" rewritten as "Yes, We Now Have Bananas."

Unfortunately, most people who tried the product did not purchase a second box. Corn flakes and freeze-dried fruit both react to the addition of milk, but not in a complementary fashion. It took about ten minutes of soaking for the fruit to properly reconstitute, at which time the corn flakes would have turned to unappetizing mush.

BREATH BLASTERS

Many products come and go leaving only a faint bad aroma to mark their passing, but none has done so as intentionally as Breath Blasters did in the mid-eighties. Breath Blasters were hollow 6-inch figures that puffed out foul smells when squeezed. The toy line was marketed by Axlon Inc., a company founded by Nolan Bushnell, inventor of the video game Pong. Designed to appeal to little boys who want to gross each other out, each character had a name befitting his particular odor: there was George Garbagemouth, Mackerel Mouth, Ms. Morningmouth, Dogbreath, Deathbreath and Victor Vomit, whose package promised "If he breathes on you, you'll want to vomit too!"

BROTHER POWER, THE GEEK; AND OTHER COMIC BOOK CATASTROPHES

Writer Joe Simon and artist Jack Kirby were two of the greatest names in comics who, in the 1940s, teamed up to give us Captain America, red-white-and-blue scourge of the Japanazis. He was clearly a hero for his times, and spawned legions of imitators. Times change, though, and later in their careers Simon and Kirby were responsible for some of the worst comic book characters ever seen.

Ask any well-informed comic book fan to name the all-time biggest comic book flop, and odds are he'll (yes, they're still all guys) suggest *Brother Power, the Geek*. This classic stinker was Joe Simon's 1968 attempt to depict the hippie movement. The cover promised "The Real-Life Scene of the Dangers of Hippieland!" in a story that owed its plot to Pinocchio. Brother Power is a tailor's dummy who is found by the "brotherly sect," a hippie group. When struck by lightning, he comes to life and gains super-powers.

The following dialogue captures the feel Simon had for contemporary slang:

Brother Nick: "Like, wow, Pow! You're a human generator! That lightning really switched you on!"

Brother Power, the Geek: "That's it, exactly! The wires that I'm strung out on are grooved with a million swinging volts!"

Brother Power's adventures were too inane to elaborate on, and his second issue, which featured Ronald Reagan and a band of missile-making hippies, was his last. He lives on only among those with an affection for the truly abysmal, along with Simon's equally short-lived *Prez*, the story of a teenager who becomes President.

Simon's former partner, Jack Kirby, achieved renown for his collaboration with Stan Lee on *Fantastic Four*, *Thor*, and *Silver Surfer*. Yet near the end of his career he came up with probably the most peculiar comic book hero ever—Paranex, the Fighting Fetus. Yes, an over-sized big-headed fetus sheathed in armor plate is featured in *Captain Planet and the Galactic Rangers* #7. He doesn't speak, but it's pretty clear where he would stand on the abortion question. Kirby also came up with Devil Dinosaur, a red Tyrannosaurus which earned this stinging critique from Beavis and Butthead:

Butthead: "Huh-huh. This sucks!....Hey Beavis, huh-huh, who'd win in a fight? Huh, Devil Dinosaur or Barney?"

Beavis: "Heh-heh-heh! Barney would kick his ass!"

Also high on anyone's list would be Phantasmon the Terrible, from Fly Man #35. This fearsome villain was gifted with the power to shoot lightning bolts from his nostrils.

BUCKMINSTER FULLER: GEODESIC DOME, DYMAXION HOUSE AND DYMAXION CAR

"A self-balancing, twenty-eight joined, adapter-base biped; an electro-chemical reduction plant, integrated with segregated stowages and thousands of hydraulic and pneumatic pumps with motors attached...guided with exquisite precision from a turret in which are located telescopic and microscopic self-registering and recording range-finders..." This is an excerpt of R. Buckminster Fuller's description of man, and it gives a feel for his unconventional perspective. An engineer, architect, ecologist and visionary, Fuller sought to unlock the laws of nature and apply them to man's technology. Under his theorem that "Intellect applied to energy equals wealth," he was convinced that real elevation of mankind's standard of living could come only if we learned to more intelligently utilize available resources. Fuller was convinced that man, as an integral part of the Universe, was not destined to fail on this planet, and he dedicated his life to developing designs and proposals toward that end.

Fuller was such an inexhaustible fountain of ideas that as a young man he was given a free tab at Romany Marie's, a Greenwich Village coffee shop, due to his ability to gather and hold a crowd. Later, *Fortune* paid him $15,000 a year just to come in occasionally and brainstorm for the editors. During the 1960s his lectures, delivered at a timed rate of 7,000 words per hour for as long as six to eight hours, drew throngs on college campuses. As the *Whole Earth Catalog*'s Stewart Brand raved, "Fuller's lectures have a raga quality of rich nonlinear endless improvisation full of convergent surprises." Houseguests found that even after he had expounded to them all evening, he might follow them into their rooms as they undressed for bed to continue making his points. Some have acknowledged that Fuller's ideas were a lot more persuasive when received in this fashion than when studied on the printed page.

Fuller is probably most famous for his design of the geodesic dome, a dome built from a network of triangles. It is light, strong, and encloses more space with less material than any other structure ever designed. A 187-foot-high geodesic dome housed the U.S. exhibit at Expo '67 in Montreal, but that application was modest compared to the uses Fuller had in mind. Because the geodesic dome retains its structural integrity at whatever size it is built, Fuller proposed a dome to cover midtown Manhattan, from river to river and from 22nd Street to 64th Street. Its base would be mounted just below the tops of the tallest sky scrapers. It would soar three-quarters of a mile above the Empire State Building, yet contain less steel than an ocean liner. In fact, it would be so light for its size that Fuller believed that by heating the air inside just a few degrees, it would pull upward against its moorings like a hot air balloon. The dome would be air-conditioned in summer, and would help retain the city's heat in winter. Heating the surface of the dome would melt off snow accumulation, and the run-off could be collected and stored in reservoirs. Fuller calculated that the dome would pay for itself within ten years with the savings in snow removal alone.

Even dismissing fantastic notions such as this, the dome has not come into the widespread use that Fuller envisioned. It is hard to maintain the faith that you have stepped boldly into the future when you're living under a leaky roof, and with the expansion and contraction of its numerous joined surfaces Fuller's dome has proven difficult to make watertight. Even *The Whole Earth Catalog*, which in earlier editions had extolled the dome, by 1981 was cautioning its readers that they would probably end up covering their domes with decidedly retro-tech asphalt shingles. Though the dome may have been efficient in concept, in execution it often proved more trouble than it was worth.

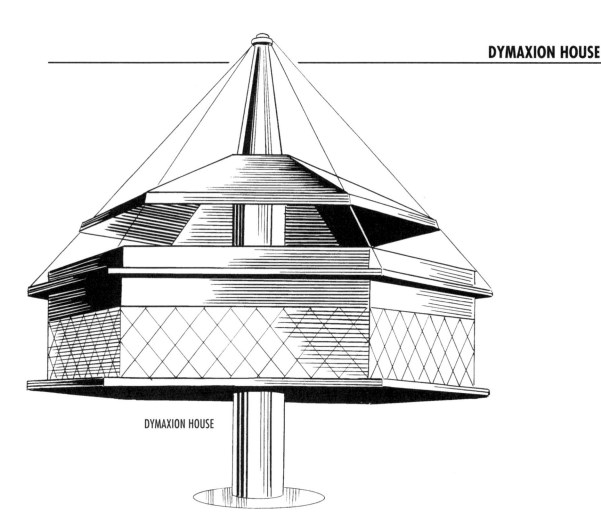

DYMAXION HOUSE

THE DYMAXION HOUSE

Of man's basic needs, housing is the one that Fuller felt had been the least improved by available technology. The cost of housing drained a disproportionate amount of a family's income, and the maintenance of a house a disproportionate amount of its time.

Conventional building technique relied upon compression—weight piled upon weight. But the strength of many materials is greater in tension than in compression, as much as twenty times greater in some steel alloys. Fuller reasoned that the best way to do more with less was through application of this principle.

The 4D (for fourth dimension) House was a single-family home in the form of a hexagonally-shaped living compartment suspended by cables from a strong, central column. The hollow column distributed light, heat, and ventilation, and was to have lenses at the top to harness solar power and a windmill to generate electricity. Rainwater drained into holding tanks in the mast, and the household water was to be filtered and reused. Solid waste was to be separated out and packaged as fertilizer. The house would be self-contained and energy self-sufficient, completely independent of electric, water or sewage hook-ups.

The sides of the house were constructed of triangles of double-paned shatterproof glass, which could be covered by roll-down steel shutters. On the flat top of the house was a fifty-foot fenced-in play area, protected by a cone-shaped aluminum roof. The inside of the house was divided into four triangular rooms and one large double-triangle, or rhomboid-shaped, living room. Floors would be pneumatic to dampen noise and to prevent injury to children.

The whole "living machine" was designed to be mass-produced like an automobile. It would come packed in crates that could be transported by truck, weigh only 6,000 pounds and sell for $1,500.

As good as this all sounds, one has to acknowledge the drawback that, to this day, the technology to realize many of these features does not exist. Undeterred by that, Fuller had additional ideas more suitable to science-fiction than to engineering. There was a "fog gun" with which you could take a shower using only a quart of water, which was then recycled. The dishwasher was expected not only to do the dishes but to put them away afterwards, an engineering detail that Fuller left for the non-visionaries to work out. Ditto for the central vacuum-and-compressed-air automatic cleaning system.

Fuller built a scale-model of his 4D House and was invited to put it on display at the Marshall Field Department Store. Their publicist pooh-poohed Fuller's "4D" name, observing that it sounded more like a failing grade or military classification than a glimpse of the future. He suggested "Dymaxion" and the name stuck. After that Fuller was regularly invited to display his

Dymaxion House and explain its principles at universities, home shows, and architectural forums. Archibald MacLeish wrote a feature on it for *Fortune*.

Nevertheless, the idea went nowhere. Even if the technical difficulties could be resolved, such a house could only be priced reasonably if it were produced in the millions. Fuller blamed resistance to his idea on self-interested architects and the hidebound construction industry; he didn't allow for the possibility that we might not all wish to live in identical houses. Huge numbers of identical units of tract housing were built in the post-World War II boom, most notably at the Levittown development in Pennsylvania. This cookie-cutter construction came in for a lot of criticism and was regarded as emblematic of fifties-style conformity. However, homeowners soon altered and individualized their homes to their own taste and needs, and such developments no longer present their original face of mind-numbing sameness. The Dymaxion Home, Fuller's perfect vision, allowed no such room for individual expression.

DYMAXION BATHROOM

THE DYMAXION BATHROOM

One element of the Dymaxion Home actually was put into limited production—the bathroom. It consisted of two compartments, tub-shower and toilet-sink, all stamped out of sheet metal. It weighed 420 pounds and was supposed to sell for about $300. Phelps Dodge built thirteen prototypes but took the project no further. Again Fuller blamed reactionaries, but even his admirers wondered whether the public would appreciate being shoehorned into the five-foot wide by five-foot tall starkness of the Dymaxion Bathroom. As one architect friend put it, "Bucky thinks people ought to get weighed sitting on a toilet seat, brushing their teeth with a cake of soap while taking a shower with a fog gun. But I ain't gonna. I just ain't gonna."

TRITON CITY

In the 1960s, with the backing of a Japanese multimillionaire, Fuller advanced plans for Triton City, a huge tetrahedronal floating building, two hundred stories high, with three base edges each 2 miles long, housing 1,000,000 people. It could be moored in Tokyo Bay, or indeed in the harbor beside any city which needed additional housing. Fuller described the structure as a sort of "bookshelf," with compartments covering the exterior which would hold individual living modules, like mobile homes. The interior of the tetrahedron would contain the utilities, vertical and horizontal transportation machinery, and a nuclear power plant which would also desalinize sea water. Despite Fuller's hopes of getting government funding behind his floating city, nothing came of it. The scale model now resides in Lyndon Johnson's Presidential Library.

And that wasn't the end of it. Fuller also questioned why we sleep in private homes and then spend our days in office buildings, where most of the same life-supporting systems are duplicated. Why not just sleep in the office buildings?, he wondered. Then there were his cloud-structure spheres, 1/2 mile in diameter, which would float over the surface of the Earth buoyed by helium gas. And so on, into the wee hours.

THE DYMAXION CAR

The Dymaxion House, as Fuller envisioned it, could be put up anywhere its owners desired, even in the most remote regions. To reach it, then, Bucky realized he must design them an appropriate vehicle—a Dymaxion Car.

Fuller got financial backing to produce his vehicle, set up shop at the old Locomobile (no kidding) Company factory building in Bridgeport, Connecticut, and hired 28 workers. The first working model rolled out of the factory doors on July 12, 1933. With its blimpish, streamlined shape, the Dymaxion Car looked like nothing else on the road until the introduction of the Oscar Mayer "Weinermobile." The driver sat at the front of the car, surrounded by windows to give him the widest possible view of the road. There was even a periscope sticking up through the roof to give him an equally good view to the rear. The car ran on three wheels, with the front two wheels providing traction and braking, the single wheel in the rear used for steering. Bucky modeled this after the rudder on a ship, arguing that the front-wheel steering of the conventional car is a mere hold-over from horse and buggy days. The Dymaxion Car could make a 360-degree turn in its own length, and thus could easily park in a space barely bigger than the car itself. The second model could seat eleven.

The Dymaxion was featured at the 1933 Chicago's World's Fair. As "the car of the future," it brought up the rear in a parade of the history of transportation. It startled the audience by speeding across the floor, then suddenly

DYMAXION CAR

stopping and performing 360-degree turns on its own axis. The crowd was sure it would flip over, but it didn't—at least not then.

It was just outside the World's Fair grounds that the Dymaxion suffered a spectacular bit of bad luck. When another car hit its rear end, the Dymaxion went out of control and rolled over. The driver was killed and the passengers seriously injured. Since the other vehicle was removed from the crash scene before reporters arrived, the immediate assumption was that the Dymaxion's radical design had proven unstable. Headlines screamed: "Freak Car Crashes" and "Dymaxion Car Kills Driver." Though Fuller built two more prototypes and continued to demonstrate the validity of the design, his hopes for large-scale production of the Dymaxion were dashed.

Although Fuller's many proposals received considerable attention in their time, remarkably little has come of them. Fuller attributed this to the inertia of vested interests, but it may be that his idiosyncratic vision was not destined for acceptance by the masses. This was a man, after all, who would criticize people for using the words "up" and "down" because such directions have no fixed meaning on a spherical planet; he insisted that "in" and "out" (of the earth's gravitational pull) were more proper terms. Fuller resigned himself to being considered a nut because he believed his ideas were fifty years ahead of their time. However, the fifty years are up now, and most of them have that quaint look that yesterday's vision of the future always does.

CALORIES DON'T COUNT

Every great diet starts with a promise that's too good to be true. No one's promises were better than those of Dr. Herman Taller. The cover of his book, *Calories Don't Count*, offers to fill the reader in on the following diet discoveries:
* Why you must never leave the table hungry if you want to be slim.
* How you can eat "almost anything" while you

watch those extra inches disappear.

* A reducing plan that includes a wide range of fried foods.

Published in 1961, the book soared to the top of the non-fiction best-seller list, though most weight-loss specialists felt it should have been forced to compete with the fictitious offerings. Taller gave the regretfully-rotund permission to consume up to 5,000 calories a day, as long as they maintained a balance of two-thirds fats, one third protein, and practically no carbohydrates at all. "Extra *slices* of chicken?" Taller asked rhetorically. "Ridiculous! I eat extra *chickens*." Of course, even those most willing to suspend disbelief might have had a problem with this, so Taller added a miracle pill to assuage their doubts: the CDC capsule. Followers of the regimen had to take two CDC (calories don't count) capsules with every meal. A month's supply of the pills could cost $600, of which Taller got a hefty percentage. The pills were nothing but safflower oil, which contains linoleic, a fatty acid that was supposed to speed the body's metabolism of fat. Dr. Taller, whose medical expertise was in obstetrics and gynecology, claimed to have lost 75 pounds with his diet. Millions of Americans, spending millions of dollars, tried to follow suit. Cashing in from every angle, Taller opened weight-control clinics in New York.

Within three months of the book's publication, the FDA obtained a court order against the CDC capsules for misleading claims. In addition to making those extra pounds melt away, the pills promised to lower and control cholesterol, prevent heartburn, improve the complexion, ward off

A revolutionary reducing plan based on the new biochemical discovery that

CALORIES DON'T COUNT

tissue. Dr. Taller explains the principles behind this new understanding of the body's chemistry and tells in full detail:

* How to eat three full meals a day and lose weight in the safest way possible.
* Why you must never leave the table hungry if you want to be slim.
* How you can eat "almost everything" while you watch those extra inches disappear.
* A reducing plan that includes a wide range of fried foods.
* How this radical new way of losing weight is linked to a low cholesterol count, better skin condition and resistance to colds and sinus trouble.

By Herman Taller, M.D.

colds and improve sexual performance. Simon & Schuster, which had sold close to a million copies of the book and would ultimately sell a million more, was forced to divert some of its profits toward litigation. In 1967 Dr. Taller was convicted on twelve counts of mail fraud, conspiracy and violation of the Federal Food, Drug and Cosmetics Act.

CANDY HALL OF SHAME

Ouch Gum, gum in the shape of band-aids, was offered by Amurol, the maker of Hubba-Bubba bubble gum. It came in strawberry, watermelon, and grape flavors, and was packaged in a metal can, just like the real thing.

Amurol also produced Squeeze Pop. The "Squeeze & Lick Lollipop" came in a clear, capped tube. Kids who like to eat toothpaste out of the tube should have gone for this artificially-flavored and colored corn syrup.

Life Savior Jesus, a Life Saver-type candy sold on a roll for 15¢, appeared in 1976. The candy wrapper contained a scriptural message.

Barfo Family Candy was introduced by Topps in 1990. The mouths of the squeezable plastic figures dispensed a sweet gelatinous substance.

Among the least successful chewing gum flavors ever marketed: banana, chocolate mint, and tangerine.

CARRIE, AND OTHER BROADWAY BOMBS

Stephen King thought it was a good idea.

The proposal had come from Lawrence D. Cohen, who had written the screenplay for the 1976 film adaptation of *Carrie*, and Michael Gore, who wrote the Academy Award-winning music for *Fame*. They had been looking for suitable material for a Broadway musical, and in a bolt of inspiration, it hit them—*Carrie*. It had an extraordinary relationship between a mother and daughter, both larger-than-life characters; it touched on primal fears and fantasies, combining elements of *Cinderella* and *Samson*; it was loaded with passion and plenty of action. They didn't see it as a *Little Shop of Horrors*, but rather "a musical tragedy belonging to the grandly serious Broadway tradition of *West Side Story* and *Sweeney Todd*," as *The New York Times* put it.

When they called Stephen King and presented their suggestion, he was silent so long that Cohen thought they had been disconnected. Then he said, "Well, if they could do a musical about a dictator

THE FRIEDRICH KURZ
RSC PRODUCTION

BETTY BUCKLEY IN CARRIE THE MUSICAL BASED ON THE NOVEL BY STEPHEN KING · MUSIC BY MICHAEL GORE · LYRICS BY DEAN PITCHFORD · BOOK BY LAWRENCE D. COHEN · WITH DARLENE LOVE · GENE ANTHONY RAY · CHARLOTTE d'AMBOISE · PAUL GYNGELL · SALLY ANN TRIPLETT · AND INTRODUCING LINZI HATELEY AS CARRIE · SET DESIGN RALPH KOLTAI · COSTUME DESIGN ALEXANDER REID · LIGHTING DESIGN TERRY HANDS · SOUND DESIGN MARTIN LEVAN · ASSISTANT DIRECTOR LOUIS W. SCHEEDER · PRODUCTION STAGE MANAGER JOE LORDEN · CASTING LYONS/ISAACSON · GENERAL MANAGER WAISSMAN AND BUCKLEY ASSOC · ORCHESTRATIONS ANDERS ELJAS · HAROLD WHEELER · MICHAEL STAROBIN · MUSIC SUPERVISOR HAROLD WHEELER · MUSICAL DIRECTOR PAUL SCHWARTZ · CHOREOGRAPHER DEBBIE ALLEN · DIRECTOR TERRY HANDS

PRODUCED IN ASSOCIATION WITH WHITECAP PRODUCTIONS INC AND MARTIN BARANDES

J THE VIRGINIA THEATRE
245 WEST 52nd STREET

DESIGNED & PRINTED BY DEWYNTERS LTD. LONDON

in Argentina or a murderous barber on Fleet Street, *Carrie* as a musical makes enormous sense. Go ahead!"

So began a seven-and-a-half-year odyssey full of false starts, delays, and problems, that finally brought *Carrie* to the Broadway stage. The production was developed in England by the Royal Shakespeare Company, which hoped to ease its debt with a success to match its *Les Misérables*. Unlike that show, though, *Carrie* did not have a successful British run to give it a boost when it crossed the Atlantic. English reviews were blistering, though some of that was attributed to resentment at seeing the revered RSC stoop to pop-Gothic gore.

The part of Carrie was played by an English unknown, Linzi Hateley, while Broadway stalwart Betty Buckley was cast as her mother. Before the show opened in New York, choreographer Debbie Allen counseled the young performers on how to handle sudden stardom. They would have been better off with advice on how to handle sudden unemployment. Advance ticket sales were small, and after opening night reviews it was clear that few more tickets would be sold. *Carrie* was burnt at the stake. Frank Rich of *The New York Times* found the song-and-dance surrounding the pig-slaughtering scene hilarious, with its ground breaking couplet: "It's a simple little gig,/ You help me kill a pig." The songs, which told 70 percent of the story, were dismissed as bubble gum. The fireworks at the prom-apocalypse, he wrote, "wouldn't frighten the Mai-Tai drinkers at a Polynesian restaurant." *Newsweek* described the concluding scene, done with smoke and lasers, as full of "sound and fury signifying silly."

Carrie closed after five regular performances. All this wouldn't be particularly notable, except that *Carrie* had managed to run up costs of about $8 million before the curtain rose on opening night. The show spent about a million for costumes, another million for the sound system, and as much again for the elaborate hydraulically-powered sets. About $500,000 was spent repainting the interior of the theater black, in keeping not only with the show's somber theme, but its somber prospects. The producers could have kept the show open a few weeks and hoped for the best but they had no cash reserves left and too little hope of profiting from any additional investment.

Rocco Landesman, the President of Jujamcyn Theaters, which had invested $500,000 and provided a house for the show, said, "This is the biggest flop in the world history of the theater, going all the way back to Aristophanes." Stephen King had a more generous view. "I liked it a lot," he said after the opening night show.

But then, it wasn't his $8 million.

Other Broadway shows whose losses rivaled *Carrie's* were *King*, the 1990 musical about Martin Luther King, which lost over $5 million in a six-week run; and *Rags*, a 1986 musical about the Jewish immigrant experience, which evaporated $5.25 million in only four performances.

New York's theater district restaurant, Joe Allen, features a wall of framed posters memorializing Broadway's greatest bombs, all of which closed on opening night or soon thereafter. Among the honorees are the oft-mentioned 1983 *Moose Murders*, a one-night stand which racked up a loss of over $1 million. The murder mystery farce, set at the Wild Moose Lodge in the Adirondacks, drowned in a sea of vitriol. *New York's* John Simon described it as "Stereo-odor-iferous smellorama...as close as I ever hope to get to the bottomless pit." Frank Rich of *The New York Times* wrote, "Will separate the connoisseurs of Broadway disaster from mere dilettantes for many moons to come..." Other titles in Joe Allen's pantheon include *Via Galactica* ("A Musical of the Future"); *Rockabye Hamlet*; *Bring Back Birdie*; *Merrily We Roll Along*; *Got To Go Disco*; *Dude*; and *End of the World*, whose poster fittingly shows a large bomb, its fuse lit, about to go off.

CELEBRITY RESTAURANT FRANCHISES, FAILED

Operating one's own restaurant is one of the most common American fantasies. It's easy to convince ourselves that the food we like, and the atmosphere we could create, would be universally appealing. This delusion is especially common among celebrities; it seems that most of them eventually decide to invest their fame and fortune in a restaurant or restaurant chain. Perhaps because of the romantic rather than practical considerations that often inspire them, restaurants have the highest failure rate of any small business, and even celebrity-owned operations are no exception. Have you dined at any of these lately?

- Alice's Restaurants. In 1969, Alice Brock planned a coast-to-coast restaurant chain based on the nationwide publicity generated by Arlo Guthrie's hit song and movie about her eatery. It would seem to have had a leg up in the marketing department, with its jingle already in everyone's mental jukebox.
- In 1969, Johnny Carson lent his name to a fast-food chain called Here's Johnny's ("Fine Food at Family Prices"). The first restaurant was opened on Johnny Carson Day in his home town of Omaha, Nebraska, a gala event which he hosted. There were plans to open a hundred more restaurants within the next eighteen months. Perhaps when he got the news that the chain flopped, he did one of those little soft-shoe routines he always did when the monologue bombed.
- Jack's Corn Crib, a chain of retail popcorn stores Jack Klugman started in 1983. It featured such flavors as root beer, cheeseburger, taco, sour cream and onion, watermelon, and pizza.

Among other losers were Willie Mays Say-Hey Restaurants, Fats Domino New Orleans-Style Fried Chicken, Tony Bennett's Spaghetti House, Broadway Joe's Restaurants, Mickey Mantle's Country Cookin', Mahalia Jackson's Glori-fried Chicken, Minnie Pearl's Chicken, and Trini Lopez Mexican Restaurants.

CIGARETTES, SMOKELESS AND OTHERWISE

What with lung cancer, low birth-weight babies, and the dangers of second-hand smoke, cigarettes have gotten a real black eye the past few decades. What's a tobacco company to do? R. J. Reynolds, which controls a third of the domestic market with its Winston, Salem, Camel, and Vantage brands, had several ideas, none of them very good.

In 1977, Reynolds noted that "all-natural" products were in vogue, so it came out with Real, the all-natural, no-artificial-additives cigarette. Marketing executives were so confident in Real that they distributed it nationally without even test-marketing it. "Through sophisticated market research techniques, we have included the consumer and his thoughts and reactions in every step of this product's development," said a confident RJR executive. "We think Real will be the most successful new brand introduction in the recent history of the cigarette business."

Others weren't so sure. They wondered, why go after the health-conscious crowd when it doesn't smoke cigarettes anyway? Most smokers couldn't care less whether their butts had additives and flavorings. After millions of dollars were wasted on advertising and distributing free samples, the brand was withdrawn in 1980. Real was a real disaster, but nothing compared to what was to come.

In 1981 R. J. Reynolds began work on a secret project,

PREMIER CIGARETTE

INSULATING JACKET   TOBACCO JACKET   FILTER

HEAT SOURCE   FLAVOR CAPSULE   TOBACCO FILTER

code-named "Project Spa." Project Spa was so secret that Tylee Wilson, president of RJR, did not even inform his board of it for five years, for fear it would leak out. What was the plan? To develop a breakthrough product, a high-tech smokeless cigarette that would silence the smoking critics, knock Marlboro out of first place, hold on to ambivalent smokers and attract abstainers.

The smokeless cigarette, named Premier, was not a normal tobacco product, but rather a sort of mechanical device to deliver the flavor and sensation of the smoking experience. Though it resembled a conventional cigarette, inside it held only a smidgen of tobacco. The smoker lit a carbon element at the front, through six tiny holes in the cigarette's end. Sucking on the cigarette then pulled hot air from the glowing ember through the pinch of tobacco and "flavor beads" housed in an aluminum capsule, which imbued the air with nicotine and a smoky taste. It then passed through a filter and into the smoker's lungs—with no smoke and no tar.

As rumors of the revolutionary new product spread, RJR's stock shot up three points. This forced a public announcement for the protection of stockholders. In September, 1987, Premier was introduced at an elaborate press conference at New York's Grand Central Station, complete with cross-sectional diagrams. Premier was touted as "the world's cleanest cigarette," and its appearance on the market was scheduled for 1988.

There were just a few problems the guys in the lab coats hadn't ironed out.

Premier was hard to light. Matches and old-fashioned lighters introduced impurities into the system, so that only butane lighters were recommended. Even so, some analysts noted that "it took a blowtorch" to get enough flame through the six little holes to ignite the carbon heating element.

Once the cigarette was lit, it was hard to get it to perform as advertised. Drawing the heated air through the system required the suction capability of an industrial vacuum. Reynolds' researchers dubbed this problem "the hernia effect."

The tube also became uncomfortably hot to hold during use.

Worst of all was its taste. Some compared it to burning plastic; the indelicate declared that "it tasted like shit" and (when lit with a match) "smelled like a fart." In tests, fewer than 5% of smokers liked its taste.

These problems might have been worked out, given enough time. But there were others intrinsic to the concept. People who smoke like the whole ritual. They like to watch their cigarettes burn, tap off the ashes, blow smoke, and see that shower of sparks in the rear-view mirror when they toss it out the car window. How could you feel like Bogey or Bacall while you strained to suck the taste of burning lettuce through a hard little plastic tube? Premier was such a different experience that it included a 4-page instruction booklet on the back of each pack. Advertisements begged smokers to "try it for a week" before making up their minds. Most who tried it wondered whether they could make it through the pack, much less the week. To top it off, it cost an additional thirty cents a pack.

There was an even stickier problem. Obviously, Premier was meant to appeal to the smoker who was worried about his health. But in the alternate reality of tobacco companies, there is no known connection between cigarettes and cancer. So how do you promote the most salient feature of your new product? Executives constantly referred to it as "a cleaner smoking experience," and the four-page booklet used the word "cleaner" no less than ten times. Smokers were expected to get the inference: cleaner means healthier. But didn't that tacitly acknowledge that the ordinary cigarettes Reynolds still sold were *unhealthy*? And as a carefully contrived device, Premier was uniquely susceptible to denunciation as a "drug delivery system" by that spoilsport Surgeon General, C. Everett Koop. Reynolds had expected its innovation to be welcomed by anti-smoking forces—

instead it was assailed as a cynical attempt to outflank them. Worse yet, critics charged that it could be easily modified to burn crack cocaine, a drug that some of them regarded as even more dangerous than tobacco. *The New York Times* was among the few who supported the product, editorializing that Premier was a step in the right direction.

Introduction of the smokeless cigarette underwent delay after delay, but ready or not, it hit the market in selected cities in October, 1988. Noting that dismal percentage who admitted to liking the taste, Reynolds' executives wistfully proclaimed that if Premier could indeed attract 5% of smokers it would be a success, after all. Four months later, Premier was pulled from the market, at a loss of $325 million. Claiming that the Reynolds Tobacco Company had learned valuable lessons from the project, a spokeswoman for the company announced that "We do not consider this to be a failure."

Learning from one's mistakes is commendable, but it shouldn't be necessary to make every possible mistake in order to do so. Nevertheless, shortly after its Premier debacle, R.J. Reynolds announced plans to test market Uptown, a cigarette specifically aimed at the African-American market. This provoked a torrent of criticism that caught RJR by surprise. "Being explicit in the targeting of any group with a product as controversial as cigarettes was a mistake," said Roy D. Burry of Kidder, Peabody. There was nothing new about targeting an ethnic market; after all, African-Americans and Hispanics buy more than half the cognac and most of the malt liquor sold in this country, and a company would be foolish not to target its best customers. It's just that the introduction of Uptown came precisely when this practice was generating a backlash. Secretary of Health and Human Services Dr. Louis Sullivan attacked RJR's plans. The director of surgery at Harlem Hospital issued a study showing that Bangladeshis lived longer than the average man in Harlem, and claimed that much of the difference was attributable to lifestyle choices, such as alcohol and tobacco use. He said that those who marketed such products were guilty of "corporate violence." Activists had already begun whitewashing over billboards for alcohol and cigarettes.

Faced with this barrage, RJR cancelled plans to introduce Uptown. Its other controversial new brand, Dakota, aimed at uneducated young women, was also pulled.

When called for information regarding Premier, RJR's public affairs spokesperson was not interested in discussing the matter. She preferred to focus attention on RJR's new *improved!* smokeless cigarette: Eclipse. We'll watch carefully.

CLEAVERS

Fate has a cruel sense of humor, and plenty of time to set up its jokes. One of its favorites is to bestow fame on people in their youth, snatch it away, then sit back and snicker with the rest of us as they spend their lives trying to regain the spotlight.

Eldridge Cleaver was a hero to sixties radicals for his prison memoir *Soul on Ice*, in which he portrayed rape as a positive political act. (It's hard to believe, but you could look it up.) Later, he joined the Black Panther Party, where he held the post of Minister of Information. Cleaver fled the United States in 1968 rather than be jailed for a shootout with police in Oakland, California. After a few months in Cuba, he moved on to Algeria, where he was to open a Black Panther "embassy." Troubles there caused him to move on to Paris. Homesick, broke, and disenchanted with Communist ideology,

Cleaver returned to America in 1975.

The fashion statement the Panthers were known for was their black berets, black leather jackets, black trousers, black shoes and black shotguns. However, Eldridge Cleaver had a new idea, equally revolutionary. Tight-fitting men's slacks with a special pouch or "appurtenance" for the male organ, called Cleavers. "There are some beautiful materials out there for women's pants but men can't wear those," Cleaver observed. "They can [wear them] in my designs since there is no mistaking that they are men's pants." Cleaver hoped that the sexual honesty of his pants would reverse the unisex trend in fashion, help reduce neuroses and inhibitions, and thereby lead to a decline in the level of violence in our society. Inspiration for Cleavers came from the codpieces adorning the male groin in 16th-century Europe. As exhibitionistic expressions, codpieces predictably grew larger and larger until they were the size of small canteloupes. Since that left a lot of room for most men, the space was used to store handkerchiefs, coins and candies.

Another former Black Panther, party chairman Bobby Seale, popped up in the mid-seventies seeking acting work in Hollywood. In 1980 he attempted to market a cookbook entitled *Barbecuing with Bobby*. Molotov cocktails to ignite those briquettes? We'll never know.

COCA-COLA COMPETITORS

Coca-Cola's immediate success spawned a slew of imitators. A presidential commission in 1908 listed 47 names of competing brands of cola. Some of them clearly infringed on the registered Coca-Cola name and were sued as a result. They include:

Afri-Cola, Ala Cola, Celery Cola, Cola-Coke, Heck's Cola, Kay Ola, Kola Ade, Kola Kola, Nerve Ola, Revive Ola, Rye Ola, Standard Cola, Wise Ola, Kike Ola, Mexicola, Pau Pau Cola, Pepsi Cola, Charcola, Cola Soda, Loco Kola, Minola, Schelhorn's Cola, Vine Cola, and Kola Pepsin.

With one notable exception, none of these offerings

managed to grab their share of the market.

7-Up also had its knockoffs, among them Lucky 7 and Upper 10 ("The *perfect* lemon-lime soda").

CORFAM

At its debut in 1964, Corfam was hailed as the most significant synthetic product since nylon and Dacron. Du Pont's artificial leather was going to do for shoes what nylon did for stockings—alter the market completely and permanently. And of course, like nylon, make Du Pont mounds of money.

Du Pont spent years developing Corfam, which *Time* magazine described as "one of the most tested and complex chemical substances ever created...it is basically a combination of polyester and polyurethane made into sheets resembling leather by an incredibly intricate process." Porous, scuff-resistant, water-repellent and shape-retaining, Corfam seemed like an ideal material for shoe uppers. It was thoroughly tested before being put on the market, with 19,000 test pairs passed out to such notorious shoe-abusers as police officers, salesmen and kindergarten kids. At the Newburgh, N.Y., plant, machines subjected the shoes to several arduous lifetimes of bending, tearing and rubbing. The tests validated Du Pont's claims—Corfam wore like armor plate.

After the exacting process of research and development, Du Pont showed the same care in the marketing of their miracle breakthrough. It was offered to an eager shoe industry—but only to the makers of higher-priced shoes. Du Pont wanted to see Corfam firmly established in the prestige market before it showed up on the racks at Woolworths.

Initial prospects looked good. Within its first two months, Corfam was available in over 100 different styles by 32 different shoe manufacturers. The pilot plant at Newburgh could not meet the demand. Corfam-producing facilities were built in Old Hickory, Tennessee, and Malines, Belgium, to supply the European market (which was being primed with a classy $2 million ad campaign). Du Pont predicted that by 1984 every fourth foot in America would be encased in Corfam. Corfam handbags, briefcases, luggage, and basketballs were in the offing. Beyond that, marketers foresaw Corfam jackets, dresses, draperies and wall-coverings. Du Pont stock rose to an all-time high.

By 1971, 100 million pairs of the synthetic shoes had been sold. Was Du Pont happy? Not very, since it had lost $100 million on Corfam. The material was expensive to make, yet Du Pont had to keep its prices below cost in order to sell it. A flood of cheap imitations had crowded Corfam out of the low-priced market, and more affluent consumers continued to prefer leather, complaining that Corfam was hot to wear and hard to break in. "Better Living Through Chemistry" was Du Pont's slogan of the sixties (one of the few points on which corporate America and the counterculture agreed), and it must have been hard for the company to face the fact that, even in the space age, they couldn't compete with a product that had been around since the late Pleistocene epoch.

Du Pont was forced to give Corfam the boot. In the early 1990s, Du Pont sold the right to manufacture the prestigious product to a company in Poland, but there too it flopped. The debacle, second in renown only to Ford's Edsel, lives on as a case study in business classes and marketing textbooks. Then again, perhaps those 100 million pairs will enjoy a useful second life a thousand years from now when our post-apocalypse progeny dig them out of landfills—still porous, scuff-resistant, water-repellent and shape-retaining.

CURTISS-WRIGHT MODEL 2500 AIR-CAR

The hovercraft, riding on a cushion of air, can traverse any reasonably smooth surface whether grassy fields, desert sands, snow and ice, swamps, rivers or open water. When its technology was first developed in the 1950s, all sorts of applications for it were seen, among them the pas-

senger vehicle. In October 1959, at New York's Rockefeller Plaza, Curtiss-Wright unveiled its Air-Car. The twenty-one-foot long, eight- foot-wide, and five-foot-high behemoth hovered a few inches off the ground on a cushion of what its makers described as "low-pressure, low-velocity" air. The *New Yorker* attended the demonstration and wrote, "Now, we don't know what the technical meaning of 'low' may be, but our term for the Air-Car's air would be 'high,' or maybe even 'gale-force,' for we noticed as we approached the Plaza that though there had been scarcely a hint of breeze along Fifth Avenue, the flags about the skating rink were violently agitated and a cornucopia of dead leaves, dust, and old lollipop sticks was swirling skyward, to the sullen whine of what might have been a battalion of outsize vacuum cleaners."

The Air-Car looked, as *The New Yorker* put it, "like a helium-happy hippo... making little, lumbering sallies at the crowd, then shy, lumbering retreats." In order to reassure the automotive consumer, the Air-Car was incongruously decorated with small, familiar touches: dual headlights and taillights, a hood ornament, a bit of chrome trim. It had a convertible roof.

The Model 2500 was driven by two aircraft engines, developing 300 horsepower. Adjustable louvers vented a portion of the compressed air to control speed and direction. Top speed was sixty miles per hour. Fuel consumption was said to be "less than a helicopter." The four-passenger Model 2500 Air-Car, planned for production in 1960, was to carry a price tag of $15,000. A two-passenger model, the Bee, was to go for about $6,000. Prices were expected to drop as demand increased.

Meanwhile, Dr. William Bertelsen, an Illinois physician, had similarly high hopes for his Aeromobile. "Since the Aeromobile needs no wheels, tires, transmission, differential, axles, brakes or suspension it should be much cheaper to manufacture than a car. Any good boatbuilder should be able to turn out a four-passenger job for less than $1500. You could drive it to lakes and go fishing." The Ford Motor Company, not to be caught unprepared was working on a Levacar.

So why don't we have the option of commuting in our Air-Cars, Aeromobiles, or Levacars? There was the noise,

high fuel consumption, and their tendency to kick up a hellacious dust storm, of course. Steering and stopping were imprecise, and while elevated on their cushion of air the hovercrafts were easily moved in any direction—a stray breeze could send them gliding uncontrollably. Big city traffic would have taken on the quality of a bumper car ride, even more so than it does now.

DEATH MAGAZINE

Al Goldstein, who made a fortune from the hard-core weekly tabloid *Screw* magazine, has occasionally attempted to broaden his publishing domain. In 1979 he launched *Death* magazine. From a marketing standpoint, it must have seemed the logical counterpoint to his sex weekly. There were articles on execution techniques, assassinations, burial practices, famous last words, freak accidents, zombies, whimsical epitaphs and notorious murderers. One photo spread showed the meticulously-piled skulls, posed skeletons and monastically-garbed mummies in the reliquary of the Church of the Immaculate Conception in Rome. An article covered the freak death of 19 residents of Boston's North End in 1919, when a 2,300,000 gallon tank of molasses burst and sent a tidal wave through the neighborhood.

There was plenty of evidence that *Death* did not take its subject too seriously. Above the title on the cover ran the line "Bigger Than Life." Lifetime subscriptions were offered for $100, the ad reading: "By the end of the 1980s, one out of every eleven people holding this magazine will be dead. What does this mean to you? Will you be ready to welcome death in style, or will you still be wearing that 1940 shroud left over from your grandfather? Will you have your application for freeze-drying on file or be buried in a pine box? Be ready to greet your maker in the latest fashion. Get a life subscription to *DEATH* and live a little." Al Goldstein's editorial in the fourth issue admits that, of the 600,000 first issues printed, only 200,000 sold. *"Death*

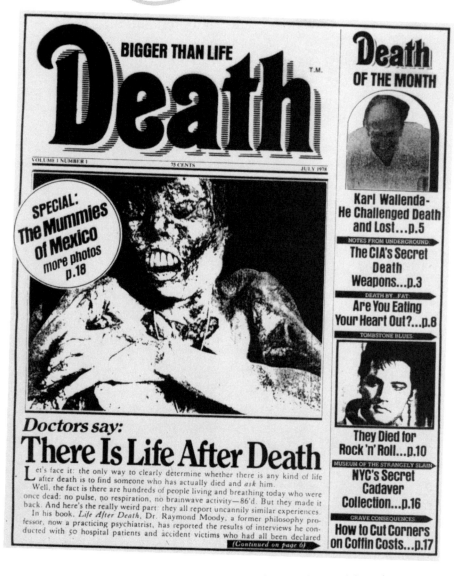

BIGGER THAN LIFE

Death

T.M.

VOLUME 1 NUMBER 1   75 CENTS   JULY 1978

SPECIAL: The Mummies Of Mexico more photos p.18

Doctors say:

There Is Life After Death

L et's face it: the only way to clearly determine whether there is any kind of life after death is to find someone who has actually died and *ask* him.

Well, the fact is there are hundreds of people living and breathing today who were once dead: no pulse, no respiration, no brainwave activity—86'd. But they made it back. And here's the really weird part: they all report uncannily similar experiences.

In his book, *Life After Death*, Dr. Raymond Moody, a former philosophy professor, now a practicing psychiatrist, has reported the results of interviews he conducted with 50 hospital patients and accident victims who had all been declared

(Continued on page 6)

Death OF THE MONTH

Karl Wallenda– He Challenged Death and Lost...p.5

NOTES FROM UNDERGROUND
The CIA's Secret Death Weapons...p.3

DEATH BY FAT
Are You Eating Your Heart Out?...p.8

TOMBSTONE BLUES

They Died for Rock 'n' Roll...p.10

MUSEUM OF THE STRANGELY SLAIN
NYC's Secret Cadaver Collection...p.16

GRAVE CONSEQUENCES
How to Cut Corners on Coffin Costs...p.17

received such a pathetic response from the public that we were not only buried, but cremated." Nevertheless, he defiantly declared his determination to keep publishing for that brave 200,000: "We will parody, satirize and scorn death because there are no options. We will stand up to death knowing that we cannot win. We will spit in death's eye, we will urinate on death's shoes... to do anything else is to be dead already."

No further issues of *Death* magazine appeared.

DINO DROP CUFFLINKS

In 1969, a company calling itself Dino Drops marketed a matching cuff links and tie tack set made from 150,000,000-year-old petrified dinosaur droppings (coprolites). Dinosaur droppings are an irreplaceable commodity, of course, but fortunately the demand never exceeded the supply.

DIRT EATING

Dirt eating is an odd, obscure, but enduring custom in the backwoods of the Deep South. Not that the vacuum cleaner bag makes a handy snack pack—any old dirt just won't do. Dirt gourmets prefer clay-rich soil dug from hillsides, often baked and then seasoned with vinegar and salt. This is called "hill dirt" to distinguish it from the grittier, rougher soil found on the Mississippi Delta, which is called "gumbo dirt." At sites from which good-tasting dirt can be dug, there are often several cars lined up as if at a drive-in bank, with people waiting to fill bags. Boxes of dirt may be mailed to relatives who have moved from the area but retain a craving for the home soil. In the early part of this century, poor rural whites were called "clay eaters" as a result of the habit.

Dirt is usually snacked upon, not eaten like a meal, at a rate of about a handful a day. The practice is most common among women, especially during pregnancy, and is related to the craving for corn starch, ashes or baking soda called *pica*. Rural doctors have noted no particular ill-effects from dirt-eating, except in the case of one patient whose large colon was impacted with the fine clay. The dirt is gathered from far enough beneath the surface to be free of chemical contaminants, insects or parasitic worms.

The New York Times reported on the phenomenon:

"It's after a rainfall, when the earth smells so rich and damp and flavorful, that Fannie Glass says she most misses having some dirt to eat.

" 'It just always tasted so good to me,' says Mrs. Glass, who now eschews a practice she acquired as a young girl from her mother, 'When it's good and dug from the right place, dirt has a fine sour taste.'"

Dirt eating is becoming less common. "In another generation I suspect it will disappear altogether, " said Dr. Dennis A. Frate, a medical anthropologist from the University of Mississippi. "As the influence of television and the media has drawn these isolated communities closer to the mainstream of American society, dirt eating has become increasingly a social taboo."

So far Mrs. Glass has felt no craving for substitutes such as baking soda or cornstarch. "Starch just don't take the place of dirt," she commented. As of the 1986 *New York Times* article, she had been off dirt for a year, after her husband complained to her that it was a bad habit "that makes your mouth taste like mud."

Still, "There are times when I really miss it," Mrs. Glass told the reporter. "I wish I had some dirt right now."

So far, dirt-eating has failed to become a widespread social trend. As a little-known aspect of the rural diet, totally organic and non-fattening, dirt seems to have real untapped potential. Maybe if it was imported from France...

DRESSES OF THE SIXTIES, FORGOTTEN

No dress concept so encapsulated the sixties sensibility as did the paper dress, covered elsewhere. However, there are a few other fadlets with which any serious student of the decade should be familiar:

Le Canned Dress. A 4 1/2-ounce texturized nylon dress that came in a pull-top can, marketed by Wippette Sportswear in 1966. Irwin Silver, the company's owner, claimed that he was "being driven crazy by cans...every time I turned around I bumped into a can.... First I saw canned candles, then canned air, and then—I wondered why dresses couldn't be packed the same way." There were three different styles available, in sizes from 5 to 13, at $25 apiece.

Do-It-Yourself Dress. Created by designer Betsy Johnson in 1966, the Do-It-Yourself dress was a clear-vinyl halter-topped shift with a zipper in back. It sold for $35, and for an extra $5 the customer received a kit of "copper coin dots, silver stars, and metallic blue rays" to glue onto the dress according to the wearer's discretion. Rudi Gernreich's model and associate Peggy Moffitt wore one to a charity ball while accompanying the designer. She had on only a red bikini bottom beneath it, though large polka dots were placed here and there as needed. Noted *The New York Times* in its coverage of the event, "some of the guests...stopped in the middle of a vigorous Charleston to crowd around Miss Moffitt for a closer look at the garment."

"I'm predicting it will replace the basic black dress," said the sly Mr. Gernreich.

Dresses for Men. With boys in long hair and beads, and all the talk of unisex, it seemed that dresses for men might be just around the corner. In 1966, a British textile manufacturer predicted that by 1980, men would be wearing skirts or kilts like those worn by the ancient Roman soldiers. Model Tony Barnes, who was photographed in a prototype, pronounced it very comfortable and practical, and predicted it would become a top male fashion. In 1967, *Time* magazine reported that apparel makers and fashion magazines were manfully trying to persuade college boys—and their dads—to skirt up for fall in kilts. New York's British Sportswear, Ltd., reported that 150 stores ordered 3,500 of their Scottish-made men's kilts. "American men are ready for something different," insisted a British Sportswear executive. *Seventeen* featured a large photo spread of kilted boys and girls at the University of Miami. *Esquire* suggested that if men were ever going to wear skirts, they would begin with the kilt. "When you come down to it, almost no man is going to wear something called a skirt," conceded a *GQ* editor, and his magazine covered the coming

DO IT YOURSELF
DRESS

63

of the kilt without ever mentioning the dreaded "s" word. The ruse did not succeed. In the eyes of American men, a skirt by any other name was still a skirt.

DRIVE-IN CHURCHES

When love is true, parting is hard. And so in the 1920s and 1930s businesses arose that did not require that Americans be parted from their cars, even for a moment. Foremost among these, of course, were the drive-in restaurants and movies.

With the drive-in movie theaters unused on Sunday mornings, the 1960s saw a new phenomena: drive-in churches. In 1967, *Time* magazine reported that over 70 were operating nationwide. Most of these placed the minister, altar, choir and organ atop the projection booth or makeshift stage. Ushers handed out hymn sheets to the worshippers as they rolled in, helped them plug in their speakers, and asked drivers to toss their donation into a bin as they left. Some even distributed communion wafers car to car. To capture the spirit of community, the con-

gregation might all roll down its windows to join in hymn-singing; coffee and doughnuts might be served at the snack bar after the service. Some pastors tried to converse briefly with congregants as they rolled out the exit; the Rev. James Hamilton of Pasadena Community Church in St. Petersburg, Florida, even encouraged his parishioners to greet visiting preachers with "a gentle, dignified horn toot."

Several churches were designed specifically for the drive-in function, the most famous being Rev. Robert Schuller's Garden Grove Community Church in California. The $3-million-dollar facility featured two twenty-five-foot-tall glass walls in front of the altar that parted when the service was about to begin, leaving only windshields between Schuller and his congregation. The mass was broadcast over the church's own channel that could be picked up on car radios. There was parking provided for 500 vehicles, as well as seats for those who chose to walk in. Schuller described it as a "twenty-two-acre shopping center for God." Disneyland's Matterhorn loomed inspirationally in the distance.

DRIVE-IN FUNERAL PARLORS

In 1968, Hirschel Thornton of Atlanta, Georgia, opened the nation's first drive-thru mortuary. It featured five picture-windows fronting on a curved, gravel driveway. Behind each window was a six-foot by twelve-foot draped and carpeted room, softly lit, with the casket tilted toward the window for easier viewing. The driveway was roofed over so that mourners would not have to peer through rain-streaked windows. Another thoughtful touch: the windows extended almost to the ground, so that drivers of low-slung sports cars would not have to unduly crane their necks. Each window had a drop-in name plate to prevent any confusion about whose remains were seen. If merely cruising by might not seem a sufficient expression of respect, a box and register was provided outside each window for written condolences.

"This will make it easier for elderly people, who can just sit in the car. There's no need to dress up this way, either," explained Thornton. "Folks will be able just to drive by and view the remains of their loved ones, and then keep going."

A few others have picked up on this approach. In 1977, the Point Coupee Funeral Home in New Roads, Louisiana, introduced a similar drive-in service, with just one viewing window. Funeral director Alvin Verrette said: "We wanted something for working people who didn't have time to dress up but who wanted to show their sympathy and give condolences. It's so nice to know someone cares." Point Coupee's window is still in service, being booked about 70 to 80 percent of the time. Irma Verrette points out its utility for bus loads of school children who might be disruptive in a parlor, or van loads of nursing home residents who might have difficulty attending a normal wake.

In the late 1980s, Gatling's Funeral Home in Chicago brought the concept thoroughly up to date. Just like at your nearby fast-food restaurant, mourners drive up to a speakerphone and press a button for service. When the mortician answers, they give him the name of their dear-departed. He presses the proper button on his control panel so that when they proceed a few feet forward to the viewing area, they see the embalmed face of their loved one appearing live (so to speak) on a closed-circuit color television screen. The picture only lasts three seconds, but a button is provided that the driver can push for repeated viewings.

The drive-by funeral has not caught on in a big way. If it ever does, a proper etiquette will presumably develop. Among other things, it will presumably frown on honking at the mourner ahead of you if he tarries, even when the line of cars is long.

EARRING MAGIC KEN

In 1993, Mattel offered Barbie's steady date in his newest incarnation—Earring Magic Ken.

"Little girls wanted Ken to look a little cooler," said a Mattel spokeswoman.

With his earring, necklace, two-toned hair, lavender fake-leather vest and pale-violet shirt, the new Ken struck a note with another group as well.

"You can't look at Earring Magic Ken and not think *gay*," Rick Garcia, director of Chicago's Catholic Advocates for Lesbian and Gay Rights, told *People* magazine. "He's stereotypically gay— it's what you saw gay men wearing a few years back. And that plastic ring that Ken wears [around his neck] looks an awful lot like what gay men were buying at sex shops."

Garcia was one of the thousands of gay men who rushed to purchase a doll that they saw as one of their own. As he told *People*, if the doll had been advertised as gay he would have protested the stereotyping, but as a doll who's still supposed to be Barbie's boyfriend, the depiction was "a hoot."

None of this was welcome news to Mattel, which professed to be amazed by the gay community's acceptance of Ken as one of their own. Some toy stores refused to carry the doll, and there were mothers who refused to buy it. As one put it, "There's no way you could sell me a Ken with an earring—it wrecks the whole all-American image."

EARRING MAGIC KEN

If you think about it, Barbie does seem like the sort of jet-setting fashion-slave that prefers the company of gay men. The question is moot, though, since neither Barbie nor Ken had the good fortune to come into the world as part of an anatomically-correct doll line.

EDISON'S CEMENT HOUSE

History shows that the most brilliant of inventors are generally not the most practical of investors. Thomas Edison often claimed that his inventive efforts were guided solely by commercial considerations, but occasionally admitted that he really "lacked the commercial temperament." When hot on the trail of a technological breakthrough, the least of his concerns was "cost-benefit" ratios. Calling a halt in the middle of a project and cutting his losses was intolerable to him.

One of the things Edison took an interest in was cement. He designed an all-steel, highly-mechanized production facility that could grind out 1,100 barrels of cement a day at a time when the average plant produced only 200. By the time the Edison Portland Cement Company was completed, it had required three years and $1.5 milion to construct, far more time and money than had been anticipated. It was clear that it would never be profitable until the demand for cement was considerably higher, but Edison insisted that he could personally create demand for its product.

Edison conceived a plan for making low-cost concrete housing, Patent No. 1,123,261, in December, 1908. The houses would be cast in one piece, using molds specially-designed by a New York architectural firm. He estimated that it would require only six hours to construct the molds and pour the concrete for a three-story, six-room home. After allowing four days for hardening, the cast-iron molds would be removed to reveal a house complete with cellar, roof, floors, walls, stairways, doors, windows, bath, pipes and conduits; only the lighting, heating and plumbing systems had to be added. If the house could be built on a site which would provide its own sand and gravel, and built in lots of one hundred or more, Edison figured the per-unit cost at $1200.

Objections were raised as to the drab monotony of such housing, but Edison claimed that decorative elements could be easily added. The real problem was cost. As the house was to be molded in one piece, the number of forms required was a daunting 2300. A builder would have to invest a minimum of $175,000 in molds and equipment, in an age when most houses were built by small contractors one or two at a time.

A few demonstration dwellings were cast near West Orange, New Jersey, but there was no interest from builders or real estate agents. Despite the unenthusiastic reception, Edison continued to improve upon it. Concrete houses should have concrete furniture, he reasoned. In addition to tables and chairs, Edison proposed making concrete refrigerators and concrete pianos, and actually cast several concrete phonograph cabinets. To marry human life to concrete in perpetuity, he even devised a concrete tombstone.

Edison continued his money-losing interest in concrete for several decades. Though the plant went through several bankruptcies, it did not close until the mid-thirties, after Edison himself had died.

Edison had several other failures in his illustrious career. One was a talking doll in the 1880s. It had an Edison phonograph built in, but the fragile device could not survive the vigorous affection of little girls. Droves of dissatisfied customers returned their broken dolls to toy stores. Edison also failed with the phonomotor, a spin-off of his phonograph. The phonomotor was supposed to harness the energy of the sound vibrations of the human voice. A sewing machine would be powered, not by a treadle or an electric motor, but by the seamstress talking in a loud voice.

In the 1920s, Edison told reporters he was working on an apparatus through which those beyond the grave might communicate with the living. He believed that intelligence was seated in billions of infinitesimal "life units" which pass from the body at the

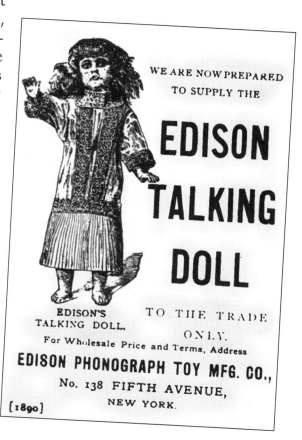

WE ARE NOW PREPARED TO SUPPLY THE

EDISON TALKING DOLL

EDISON'S TALKING DOLL.

TO THE TRADE ONLY.

For Wholesale Price and Terms, Address

EDISON PHONOGRAPH TOY MFG. CO.,

No. 138 FIFTH AVENUE, NEW YORK.

[1890]

time of death and eventually enter other bodies. Edison believed that a powerful amplifier might make audible their weak vibrations. He gave interviews on the subject, and articles appeared with titles such as "Edison Working on How to Communicate with the Next World," and Edison 'Spirit Finder' Seeks Great Secret." The public took the project very seriously, as there was enormous confidence in Edison's genius. "Ten million men and women who have lost dear ones in the war are hungering for word or knowledge as to the existence of life after the life we know," wrote one interviewer. As the apparatus failed to materialize, Edison's responses to questions about it grew testy. When asked how the machine would work, he responded, "What difference does that make? There are half a dozen ways of making a machine or of approaching the problem." Eventually he called an end to inquiries by claiming the whole matter had been a joke.

THE EDSEL

It is hard to think of another product, flop or otherwise, that started out with higher hopes than the Edsel. At the outset of the fifties, Ford Motor Company executives felt that they had a gap in their product line. Fords were attracting the first-time buyer, and Lincoln did well in the luxury class. But as middle class consumers had more money to spend, many were trading up not to Ford's medium-priced Mercury, but to Oldsmobiles, Buicks and Dodges. To capture this market, a whole new division of the Ford Motor Company was created in 1952.

Ford management felt that starting from scratch gave them a unique opportunity to create a fresh, enticing image for the new line, untainted by prior associations. Car as Practical Means of Transportation was subordinated to the quest for Car as Ego Extension and Status Symbol. As one executive put it, "We said to ourselves, let's face it—there is no great difference in basic mechanism between a two-thousand-dollar Chevrolet and a six-

thousand-dollar Cadillac. Forget about all the ballyhoo and you'll see that they are really pretty much the same thing. Nevertheless, there's something—there's *got* to be something—in the makeup of a certain number of people that gives them a yen for a Cadillac...something that has nothing to do with the mechanism at all but with the car's personality, as the customer imagines it. What we wanted to do was give the [Edsel] the personality that would make the greatest number of people want it."

Originally the project was known as the "E-Car"—E for experimental. Richard Krajve, manager of the new division, suggested that the car be named after Edsel Ford, the only son of Henry Ford, who had died in World War II. President of Ford for 24 years, Edsel had turned his father away from the company's stark, utilitarian designs, and helped bring about the sleekly-styled Lincoln Continental of the late 1930s. His sons demurred, feeling that their father might not have cared to see his name spinning on a million hubcaps, and suggested that an alternative be found. Research outfits fielded an army of interviewers to evaluate the public's reaction to a wide variety of names—and not only the names, but each name's opposite, on the theory that there was a subliminal association between a word and its antonym. Still not satisfied, the market research department commissioned ideas from the prominent American poet Marianne Moore with the following guidelines: "We should like this name...to convey, through association or other conjuration, some visceral feeling of elegance, fleetness, advanced features and design." Among her suggestions, later printed in the *New Yorker* and still later, in book form: "Mongoose Cigique", "Pastelogram", "Pluma Piluma", "Andante Con Moto", "Utopian Turtletop", "Turquoise Cotinga", "Resilient Bullet", "Intelligent Bullet" and "Bullet Cloisonné." Ford rejected these and next commissioned its ad agency to come up with the elusive moniker. It compiled a list of eighteen thousand possibilities, including Zoom, Zip, Henry and Drof (spelled backwards is...). They pared the list down by two-thirds and proudly presented it to a stunned Krajve. "We don't want six thousand names," he gasped. "We only want *one*." In frustration the company finally returned to the name Edsel (Old English, "From the rich man's house"), and the Ford brothers acquiesced. There was a double irony in the choice. After its Herculean effort to find the perfect name the company, in exhaustion, ended up choosing one that tested poorly with customers. Secondly, there is the fact that, unlike his namesake, Edsel Ford was known for his impeccable taste.

In order to generate the greatest possible attention for the Edsel after its long, drawn-out publicity campaign, Ford unveiled the 1958 Edsel in the summer of 1957. It came in four main models, at different prices: the Corsair, Citation, Pacer, and Ranger. The television commercial proclaimed: "They'll know you've arrived when you drive up in a 1958 Edsel, the car that's truly new from nameplate to taillights."

Its styling was certainly distinctive, especially viewed

head on. Set far to either side were twin pairs of headlights that bugged out like the eyes of a crab. Beneath them was a bifurcated, horizontal grille that sat well back of the heavily-chromed, jut-jawed bumper. In the center of it all, the *pièce de résistance* (or was it the *coup de grace?*): the vertical 'horsecollar' grille. Intended to evoke the classic look of the 1930s Packards, the grille merely added another sour note to the cacophonous din of the front end. It has been compared to everything from an Oldsmobile sucking a lemon to a toilet seat to something even less polite.

The "advanced engineering" that the publicity had promised turned out to be little more than a few mechanical gimmicks. There was the "drum-like speedometer that glows a menacing red when the car exceeds a preset speed" (Ford's description). The automatic transmission was controlled by buttons set in the center of the steering wheel, the "Teletouch Drive." Drivers found the system inconvenient, especially since the buttons in many of the cars couldn't be budged without a ball-peen hammer. In fact, far from realizing the consumer's dreams, early Edsels were a nightmare of oil leaks, sticking hoods, faulty power steering, sloppy trim, peeling paint, and electrically-operated trunks that wouldn't open. An executive later estimated that only half of the first Edsels performed properly.

1957 was a year that bombarded car buyers with the

chrome-laden, rocket-styled, shark-finned Cadillacs, Oldsmobiles, Chryslers and Dodges that social critic Lewis Mumford called "those fantastic and insolent chariots." By the the time the Edsel appeared the appetite for novelty had been thoroughly gorged, and its distinctive styling became an immediate joke. 1957 was also the beginning of a recession and a slump in auto sales. Despite all the planning and research, the Edsel arrived a few years too late. The new boom was in compact car sales, an area that Ford's research had overlooked completely. (This was the period when the Volkswagen "Beetle" got a firm foothold in the U. S. market.) The Edsel line was continued for three years, with lower prices and more conservative styling each year. Nevertheless, sales continued to fall. Only 3,008 of the nondescript 1960 model were produced, and Ford ended the line having sold only 111,009 in all. So much for the fears of Edsel's name "spinning on a million hubcaps." So many were given away in promotions that it was common for Edsel owners to greet each other with, "Where did you win yours?" There were compensations, of course. It is claimed that during its three years of production only one Edsel was ever reported stolen.

BY 1960, THE HUMBLED EDSEL GAVE UP ITS SIGNATURE GRILLE.

The Edsel lost between $250 to $350 million, making it the biggest debacle in automotive history to that point. It also gave a black eye to the kind of motivational research that probed consumers' deepest yearnings, but never asked them what they thought about price, cost of upkeep, insurance rates, and cars too long to fit in garages. The semanticist S.I. Hayakawa wrote that in Ford's efforts to put out a car that would satisfy people's sexual fantasies, they had neglected what he called the "reality principle." "The trouble with selling symbolic gratification via such items as...the Edsel...is the competition offered by much cheaper forms of symbolic gratification, such as *Playboy* (fifty cents), *Astounding Science Fiction* (thirty-five cents), and television (free)."

Ironically, its peculiar history has lent the Edsel a kind of perverse glamor. Yesterday's ugly ducklings are today's prized collector's items. A 1960 Edsel Ranger Convertible that originally sold for about $3,000 recently sold for $42,000.

ESPERANTO

"What we have heah is a faileah to *communicate*," the prison warden in *Cool Hand Luke* was fond of saying. Sometimes that seems to be the problem of the human race, with over three thousand different languages. In 1887 Dr. D. L. Zamenhof of Warsaw announced a solution: Esperanto, a language which he expected to be adopted universally.

To make it easy for people of different nationalities to learn, Esperanto ("One who hopes") was kept as simple as possible. The vocabulary is derived from the Romance (Latin-based) languages. Spelling is phonetic, the pronunciation of each letter is consistent, and there are no silent letters. Only 16 rules of grammar have to be learned. All nouns end in o, all adjectives in a, and all adverbs in e. Plural nouns end in oj, pronounced "oy." Unlike most European languages, nouns have no assigned gender, and there is only one definite article, la. Verbs are all regular and have only one form for each tense. A sentence in Esperanto might read: "La internacieco de la scienco nerezisteble postulas la internacieco de la lingvo." ("The internationality of science irresistibly demands the internationality of language.")

Zamenhof's book *Fundamento de Esperanto*, published in 1905, laid out the principles of the language. The same year marked a high point for his language, with 15 international congresses drawing five thousand enthusiasts from 43 different countries. All participants at the congresses spoke Esperanto, and even the entertainment—plays, opera, vaudeville skits—was performed in the international language. One tour de force was to stage a play in which every actor was chosen from a different country. It was claimed that such performances, with every participant speaking fluidly in Esperanto and the international audience effortlessly taking it all in, proved its potential.

Instant worldwide communication and almost-as-instant worldwide travel would seem to validate Zamenhof's belief that such a language was needed. And World War I convinced many that any efforts to promote international understanding and communication were worthwhile. So what happened?

For one thing, Esperantists did slightly exaggerate their ability to effortlessly comprehend each other. National accents make uniform pronunciation difficult. While the language was intended to be international, it is obviously much easier for Italians and Spaniards to learn than for Japanese and Iraqis, since it is based in European languages. To be fully implemented it could not be optional—nations would have to force it upon their citizens. Much of a nation's sense of identity is bound up in its language, and efforts to change a nation's tongue have at times led to revolution.

The internationality of Esperanto raised suspicions in certain quarters. Adolph Hitler wrote in *Mein Kampf* that Esperanto was a Jewish plot (surprise, surprise) to break down national sovereignty so that Jews could more easily run things. Others claimed it was part of International Communism's plans for world domination. Once everyone spoke the same language, communist propaganda could be spread more easily. After Germany conquered Poland, the Gestapo were given orders to round up the Zamenhof family. The founder of Esperanto had died in 1917, but his son and two daughters, who had carried on his work, died at the hands of the Nazis. With war hysteria also came suspicions that Esperantists were using the language as a secret code for international spy-rings, and practitioners were persecuted until the end of the war.

There are still Esperantists among us. They wear little green stars in their lapels when traveling so that they can recognize each other. The Universala Esperanto-Asocio (founded in 1908) has members in 83 countries and claims some 100,000 people can speak the language. The Esperanto League for North America (founded in 1925) has a membership of 825. There are more than 30,000 books and 100 periodicals published in Esperanto, including the works of Shakespeare, Norman Mailer, Agatha Christie and Mao Tse-tung. There are even Braille books in Esperanto.

It was the belief of Dr. Zamenhof and his disciples that a common language would end war, that people who could readily communicate with each other would not resort to violence. Many of us, though, have our doubts. After all, domestic violence occurs between people who communicate all too frequently.

FALLOUT SHELTERS

On July 25, 1961, President Kennedy delivered a televised speech that was the equivalent of yelling "Fire!" in a crowded theater. The Russians, he told an audience of 50,000,000, were threatening to cut off American access to the free city of Berlin, and if they used force we would respond in kind. In other words, nuclear war was a looming possibility. "In the event of an attack, the lives of those families which are not hit in a nuclear blast and fire can still be saved if they can be warned to take shelter and if that shelter is available," said the President. "We owe that kind of insurance to our families and to our country...the time to start is now."

Before that speech, bomb shelters were identified with the sort of cranks who worried about fluoride in the water supply. After the speech they were a national mania. The Eisenhower-era pamphlet, *Family Fallout Shelter*, which had been collecting dust for years, went into multiple printings—22,000,000 were eventually distributed. Civil Defense officials, once as lonely as the Maytag repairman, found themselves in great demand as public speakers. Children practiced "duck and cover" drills at school and learned about do-it-yourself shelters at Boy Scout Cavalcades. One such tip: an improvised shelter could be set up in a hurry under a table covered with dresser drawers filled with bricks. "Be careful not to overload the table to the point where it will collapse," warned the official instructions helpfully. The *Library Journal* had a helpful one called "Bomb Shelter Books," *American City* advised on "How To Zone for Fallout Shelters," and *Fortune* assured its readers "Economy Can Survive Nuclear Attack."

Whether the economy could survive a nuclear attack may have been debatable, but that it could profit from nuclear fears was not. The survival business was predicted to have a potential of from $2 billion to $20 billion. One Wall Street firm advised investors that "...this industry could rival in magnitude other well known federally-sponsored programs such as road building and urban renewal." While many families took the do-it-yourself route, walling-off a section of the basement according to plans printed in *Popular Mechanics*,

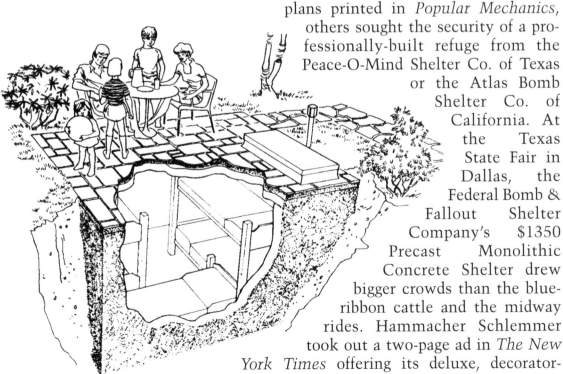

others sought the security of a professionally-built refuge from the Peace-O-Mind Shelter Co. of Texas or the Atlas Bomb Shelter Co. of California. At the Texas State Fair in Dallas, the Federal Bomb & Fallout Shelter Company's $1350 Precast Monolithic Concrete Shelter drew bigger crowds than the blue-ribbon cattle and the midway rides. Hammacher Schlemmer took out a two-page ad in *The New York Times* offering its deluxe, decorator-designed "Shelters for Living," at $20,000 installed. A newspaper ad warning "Everyone Is a Target!" sold 236 Fox Hole Shelters in a month. "My best salesmen are Kennedy and Krushchev," crowed one happy entrepreneur. When asked whether his company guaranteed its product, one shelter salesman shrugged, "Well, what's the difference? They won't be coming around to complain if it doesn't work."

As a matter of fact, many of the shelters did not wait until a nuclear war to prove themselves unreliable. One Dallas woman paid $2,500 to have an underground prefabricated steel shelter installed, only to have its roof cave in after the first heavy rain. Others found their shelters regularly flooded with water that, after a nuclear attack, would have been a radioactive broth. Owner-built shelters had their own problems. Dr. Willard Libby of the Atomic Energy Commission tried to prove that protection could be had for as little as $30 when he constructed a backyard shelter from sandbags, plastic sheeting, and two-by-fours. It was later reported to have burnt up in a small brush fire.

Along with the fallout shelters, there was money to be made selling the supplies to stock them. "Survival stores" carried hand-operated ventilation pumps, chemical toilets, filters, flashlights, first aid kits, and food and water packaged for long-term storage. It seemed that almost every product could claim to be necessary equipment for World War III. Camping equipment was hyped as "survival gear."

A crowbar was sold as an instant shelter, useful for opening any nearby manhole cover. Women's shops promoted shelterwear, recommending "bright, warm, comfortable things," for example, "gay slacks and a dress with a cape that could double as a blanket." And of course, guns.

Picture it: you're safely locked behind your blast-proof doors, surrounded by your two-week supply of canned food, bottled water, garbage-pail toilet, and battery radio tuned to CONELRAD. Suddenly, there's a frantic banging at your door. Your neighbor, who had gaily fiddled while you grimly prepared, wants in. What to do? Share your precious supplies and risk running out? Religious leaders weighed in on both sides of the issue, some feeling that the true Christian would get out of his own shelter in order that his neighbor might use it; others argued that sharing your shelter was the equivalent of squandering your family's resources—"irresponsible charity." For most fallout shelter owners, the dilemma came down to this: should I blast him with the 12-gauge, or pepper him with the .22? In fact, the to-shoot-or-not-to-shoot debate was carried on with such relish that some observers suspected that the main appeal of owning a fallout shelter was the opportunity it might provide to blow away pesky neighbors. Frederick E. Jessett, an Episcopalian clergyman, satirically suggested in *Christian Century* that the true survivalist get a head

FROM THE US GOV'T PUBLICATION "THE FAMILY FALLOUT SHELTER"

The radioactivity of fallout decays rapidly at first. *Forty-nine hours after an atomic burst the radiation intensity is only about 1 percent of what it was an hour after the explosion. But the radiation may be so intense at the start that one percent may be extremely dangerous.*

Therefore, civil defense instructions received over CONELRAD or by other means should be followed. A battery-powered radio is essential. When radiation meters suitable for home use are available they will be of value in locating that portion of the home which offers the best protection against fallout radiation. There is a possibility that battery-powered radios with built-in radiation meters may become available. One instrument thus would serve both purposes.

Your local civil defense will gather its own information and will receive broad information from State and Federal sources. It will tell you as soon as possible:

How long to stay in your shelter.
How soon you may go outdoors.
How long you may stay outside.

You should be prepared to stay in your shelter full time for at least several days and to make it your home for 14 days or longer. A checklist in the Appendix, (page 30) tells what is needed. Families with children will have particular problems. They should provide for simple recreation.

There should be a task for everyone and these tasks should be rotated. Part of the family should be sleeping while the rest is awake.

To break the monotony it may be necessary to invent tasks that will keep the family busy. Records such as diaries can be kept.

The survival of the family will depend largely on information received by radio. A record should be kept of the information and instructions, including the time and date of broadcast.

Family rationing probably will be necessary.

Blowers should be operated periodically on a regular schedule.

17

start and shoot his neighbors as soon as possible, just to be on the safe side.

By early 1962, the boom had gone bust. *Time* magazine reported that six hundred fallout shelter businesses had gone bankrupt. One dealer who had been receiving 40 calls a month received just one. Contractors who had switched from installing swimming pools to installing shelters went back to their old line of work. It was "a real loused-up deal," as one manufacturer put it. People just got tired of the crisis, doubted that war would come, and wondered if they really wanted to survive it if it did. And when it came to spending an average of $2,000 on a fallout shelter—well, as Walter Karp wrote in *American Heritage*, most Americans experienced "shellout falter." Despite the high profile of the craze, precious few fallout shelters were actually built.

Within a few years, those fallout shelters that had not caved in or filled up with stagnant water were being used as teenage hangouts, mushroom farms, or as storage for old tires and bicycles. Stale vitamin-packed "Fallout Biscuits," unpalatable at the best of times, were tossed out. A Massachusetts doctor told *Newsweek* that people called him a fool when he built his shelter. "And now I guess I was," he admitted. Said a Chicago housewife, "If a bomb fell, I'd rather run outside than in there, it's so dirty."

The new emphasis was on community shelters rather than individual ones, though once again the concept seemed dubious. In one 1967 civil-defense experiment in Athens, Georgia, 750 volunteers entered a simulated fallout shelter for the weekend. Before the weekend was up, 669 had chosen to take their chances outside. One of them explained: "We weren't told what to expect. We didn't know we'd have just biscuits and water or we'd have brought food. We didn't know we'd be sleeping on the floor for two days." Ah, that indomitable pioneer spirit.

In the seventies, a new plan for nuclear survival was promoted, even more foolish than the shelters. In the event of nuclear war, Americans were to relocate to designated rural areas by car. One local civil defense official, asked if he thought the plan was workable, admitted that he found it hard enough getting home in rush hour traffic let alone in a panic-fueled mass exodus. Families were expected to bring all necessities with them, and organization was limited to the issuance of such strictures as "No alcohol, drugs, or firearms may be taken to relocation areas." When asked who would run the camps once people got there, the official mused, "I don't know—probably the ones who brought their alcohol, drugs, and firearms."

FANNY WRAPPERS

Look through a few hundred old magazines and you'll come across some strange things. Things you've never seen before, and never even heard of. Things that were going to be really, really big.

In the 1970s, Sonya Riekel's influence on mass fashion was being compared to that of Coco Chanel—she had introduced the "poor boy" look and tent dresses of the 1960s; sold to Jackie Onassis, Catherine Deneuve and Lauren Bacall; and ran an $11 million empire. So when *Newsweek* went to her boutique on the Left Bank in Paris to cover her new line, it was with a sense that it was getting a sneak preview of the next big thing. That big thing was the "fanny-wrapper," a foot-wide tube of cloth worn tightly over the hips of a midi-length dress. Models strutted up and down the runway wearing it in combination with a leather Sam Browne belt. The look "was a show-stopper," and one veteran fashion photographer

FANNY WRAPPER

82

is described putting down his camera, "claiming he was too overwhelmed by the sensuality of it all to continue." *Newsweek* informed us that Seventh Avenue copy shops were already busily knocking off the fanny wrapper. Serves them right.

FLAT EARTH RESEARCH SOCIETY

Once universally accepted, the assumption that the world is flat has been seriously undermined in the past five hundred years. There are still those have not yet caved in, however, and their view is supported by the ongoing work of the Flat Earth Research Society. It collects and reports evidence that the world is, as common sense tells us, flat and does not move. Its map of the earth shows it to resemble a phonograph record with the North Pole at the center and the continents radiating out from around it. The outer edge of the world is circled by the antarctic ice cap.

The society attracts mainly religious fundamentalists of the type who would consider Pat Robertson a secular humanist. Flat Earthers call themselves "Zetetic," or characterized by a seeking of truth and a denial of "imaginary" theories, to distinguish themselves from "Globularists," who believe that the world is round, and would obviously fall for anything. They regard science as a religious cult, fanatical in the extreme. As their literature puts it, "We maintain that 'scientists' consist of the same old gang of witch doctors, sorcerers, tellers of tales, the 'Priests-Entertainers' for the common people. 'Science' consists of a weird, way-out occult concoction of gibberish theory-theology...unrelated to the real world of acts, technology and inventions, tall buildings and fast cars, airplanes and other Real and Good things in life..."

One of the foundations of their belief is that when Jesus Christ descends from the Heavens at the time of the rapture, He must be visible to all of the world's humanity at the same time. They have scientific evidence as well, drawn from various nineteenth- century surveying experiments conducted by British Flat Earthers. They also ask why, if the world spins, does a cannon ball fired straight up not return to earth miles away rather than nearby? The society publishes the *Flat Earth News* which, to its credit, has some very kind things to say about Elvis.

FLYING CARS

A flying car is the sort of thing we expect crackpot inventors to busy themselves with, and for most of this century they have. Mating the automobile and airplane makes sense, right? You have your wheels for gadding about town and when there's a longer trip, snap on the wings, rev up the propellor, and take off. Just the sort of progress the twentieth century was supposed to deliver.

The first serious design came in 1917, exhibited at New York's Pan-American Aeronautic Exposition by renowned aircraft designer Glenn Curtiss. The three-seat flying car did fly, but poorly, and Curtiss returned his efforts to conventional aircraft. Next on the scene was the Aerobile, or Arrowbile, of 1937, designed by aviation pioneer Waldo Waterman. Studebaker was sufficiently impressed with the Aerobile to consider selling it through their dealer network, but plans fell through. In 1939, Juan de la Cierva introduced a roadable variation of his successful autogyro design, the Pitcairn P-36 Whirlwing. Nothing came out of this one either.

At the end of World War II the aircraft industry, which had geared up for wartime production, was looking for civilian applications of its expertise. It was predicted that private ownership of planes would be as common at the end of the 1940s as private ownership of cars had been in the 1930s. At the same time, the market for conventional light planes was flooded with military surplus, so customers had to be attracted by something else. America was riding a wave of optimism about a prosperous future

in which all technological obstacles could be overcome., and flying cars seemed like a natural part of the landscape. A plethora of designs came out, including George Spratt's Controllable Wing Car in 1945, the Fulton Airphibian (probably the best name of the bunch), George Hervey's Travelplane of 1947, the Whitaker-Zuck Planemobile also of 1947, and Moulton Taylor's Aerocar, on the drawing table from 1949 to the mid-1970s. Of all the designs, the one that came closest to fruition was the Hall Flying Car.

In 1945, Ted Hall quit his position as Chief Research Engineer at Consolidated Vultee Aircraft in San Diego to pursue his dream of designing flying cars for the common man. With another Consolidated Vultee alumni, Tom Thompson, he built his first prototype. Since they had no forms or tooling, their works pounded lightweight sheet aluminum into the proper shapes with rubber mallets over sandbags. The finished sections were then attached to a tubular-steel frame. The propeller was attached to a shaft that stuck out at the point where a hood ornament might normally be. Painted black and with its pinched, aerodynamic front end, it looked like something Batman could use. Attaching the wings and twin-boom tail assembly took four mechanics ten minutes. It was a three-wheeler and sat two passengers. The car alone weighed 938 lbs., assembled to fly it

PILOTED BY MRS. TAYLOR, THE INVENTOR'S WIFE, AEROCAR TAKES OFF AT 50 MPH, HAS ENOUGH FUEL FOR 300 MILES

IS IT A CAR? OR IS IT A PLANE?

It is both: a convertible creation that travels on land and in the air

A plane that can proceed to its destination when grounded and a car that can fly when traffic-bound, the Aerocar is a new convertible machine invented by ex-Navy Pilot Moulton B. Taylor of Longview, Wash. Other trial flying cars have always had to leave their wings and tails at the airport, but Aerocar hauls them right down the highway. Approved by both the highway commission and CAA, Aerocar can do 60 mph on land without its trailer, 50 mph with it attached, and can fly 100 mph at altitudes up to 12,000 feet. Taylor has already built five custom models and is negotiating to have the two-way vehicle mass-produced

CONVERTING CAR to plane, Mrs. Taylor attaches wings and tail. She finished job in 10 minutes but it can be done in five.

TRAVELING BY LAND. Aerocar pulls trailer made of its sports coupe. Its 143-hp engine is located in the back of

weighed 1,860 lbs., or about 750 lbs. more than a comparable aircraft. It had a 30-foot wingspan and its 130-hp engine could deliver 110 mph in the air, 60 mph on the ground. After the Hall Flying Car was successfully test flown in 1946, it was featured in *Popular Science*, *Scientific American*, and *Life* magazine. Hall's former employer, now renamed Convair, bought the concept. The company was so confident in its commercial appeal that they bought up the Stinson Aircraft Company and the Stout Aircraft Company (manufacturer of the Skycar) to help them produce and market it. They thoroughly revamped the design, mating a conventional-looking four-wheel car to a wholly-detachable flying apparatus, and called it the ConVairCar. It resembled a Piper Cub mounting a Plymouth. Convair expected to sell 160,000 of them at $1500 a piece, with an additional charge for the flying attachment. The flying attachment would also be available for rent at airports nationwide, so it would not be necessary to buy one's own. The company believed that it would sell a lot of ConVairCars to traveling salesmen.

The original protoype logged over 100 flying hours. After one flight a highway patrolman pulled into the landing field, looked over the vehicle, and said it was either time for him to get a new book for writing tickets for flying cars, or else change his brand of liquor.

Unfortunately, on one test flight the pilot misjudged his fuel supply and was forced to make an emergency landing on a dirt road. Roadside trees sheared his wings off, and the fiberglass body of the car was badly damaged. The resulting bad publicity caused Convair to shelve its plans to market the vehicle.

In 1973, *Flying* featured the scariest flying car of all—a flying Ford Pinto, of exploding gas tank fame. The wings, tail, and aircraft engine with pusher propellor were a single unit which slid onto tracks on the roof of the car. Normal take off was done with propellor power alone, but it was possible to give it a running start with the Pinto. Production was scheduled for 1975, the complete package going for just under $18,000. The article concludes with that battle-cry of the crackpot inventor, "Remember, they laughed at the Wright brothers too."

When the flying Pinto crashed on a test flight, the project was cancelled.

Flying cars still show up in *Popular Mechanics*, one as recently as 1994. Called the Aircar, this newest design features "low aspect ratio" wings, like a paper airplane. With a mere 10-foot wingspan, it's not necessary for the wings to be removed to make the Aircar street legal.

All of the flying car concepts suffered from the same drawbacks. The result of the hybrid would always be an unfortunate compromise: not much good as a car, not much good as a plane. In the air it had to carry the weight of its automobile running gear. On the ground it was too lightly built for safety, with poor road-hugging aerodynamics. Then there was the cost. At the time most of these designs were floated, surplus planes were available for far less than the cost of any proposed flying car—and they flew a lot better, too. And what were you supposed to do with the wings when you took them off after flying somewhere? Since you couldn't land these contraptions just anywhere, why not simply fly commercially, then rent a car?

Perhaps it's just as well that the concept never took off. It would make running out of gas a whole new experience. And would you want to meet the same jerk who cuts you off on the freeway at 5,000 feet? Flying the family car over the sunny Southwest sounds great, but how about a rush-hour traffic jam over Chicago when a storm blows in? Would we have air traffic controllers every ten miles to supervise travelers, or would it be a free-for-all?

Even if you survived the flight, the liability insurance would probably kill you.

FOAM HOMES

In the sixties, a lot of questions were asked that had never been raised before. Like why get some suit-and-tie job when you could sell homemade candles? Why spend

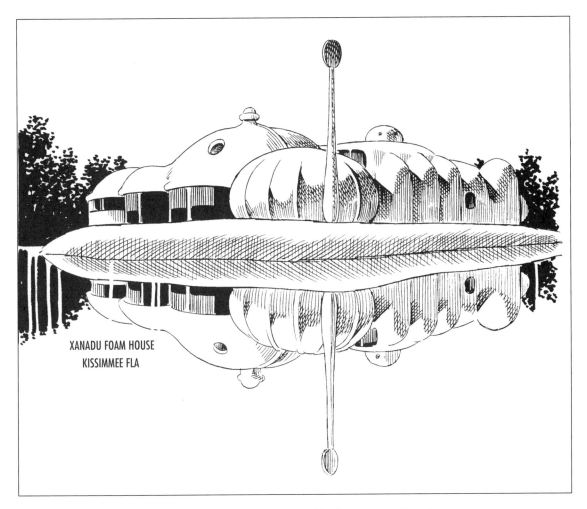

XANADU FOAM HOUSE
KISSIMMEE FLA

money on groceries when there was all this great food in the dumpsters behind supermarkets? And why live in some boring bourgeoise box instead of an old school bus, a teepee, or—a house created from polyurethane foam? Most of these questions have been answered satisfactorily by now, including the one about foam homes.

Polyurethane foam is created by mixing two liquids that, when combined, expand thirty times in volume and form a cellular structure that quickly dries and hardens. Once pressure guns were invented to spray the foam as an insulating material, architects began to see its potential as a building medium. Sprayed five-to-eight-inches-thick over simple forms, the foam hardened to become a self-supporting shell. This seemed to offer a dramatic step forward in shelter construction—rather than put up a structure and then insulate it, you could build a structure out of the insulation itself. For protection against ultraviolet rays (which deteriorate it), it could be covered with a thin layer of plaster or concrete.

A 1971 article in *Vogue*, "Blow Me A House," claimed that "there is no turning back from the apparent good sense of the material." It enthused over the possibilities: "This astonishing material has extraordinary properties of hardness, durability, and versatility. It can be sawed, carved, painted...It can be cut, patched, refoamed...It never gets termites or mildew...For insulation—warm in winter, cool in summer—it is unbeatable. Sound-and weatherproof, it is fire-resistant. Above all, it allows complete freedom of form and expression, unlimited choice of sculptural shapes, curves, proportions, scale unknown to standardized building...Aesthetically it's like living in a free-form sculpture...Even the furniture—a great saving—can be foamed in."

A reporter for *Life* magazine compared the appearance of a foam house she visited to "an Olympian soufflé or a giant mushroom with portholes." Inside, she found that "To one raised in the tradition of flat planes and right angles, being released to this gentle whoosh of ellipse and flowing space is mildly intoxicating. One visitor complained that every time she looked out the window the countryside appeared to be moving...but others, especially children, like the sensation of movement and, finding it hard to deny the house's natural choreography, dance happily wherever they go." (Yes, but in the sixties you ran into happily dancing children everywhere.)

Bob Masters and Roy Mason were early pioneers and enthusiastic proselytizers of foam construction. Most foam construction was based on chicken-wire forms, but they sprayed foam onto the inside of giant vinyl "balloons" to create organically-rounded rooms. To promote the concept, they began building showcase "homes of the future" around the country. The homes carried the name

"Xanadu," which is also the title of Mason's book on the concept. The outlandish domed-and-spired constructions, opened for public tours, demonstrated the unlimited possibilities of polyurethane foam.

So why aren't foam houses everywhere? For one thing, they weren't as cheap as they looked. They might have become cheap if millions of people had wanted them, but they didn't. Then there were the imponderables. As in any new technologies, the first purchasers are basically guinea pigs. They're the one's who'll discover the major flaws in the concept. There was a health scare in 1980 with the ureformaldehyde foam which was being sprayed into houses as insulation, and which had been used in some foam homes. Foam can be formulated without formaldehyde, but who knows what problem will show up next? We take on a thirty-year mortgage with the assumption that our house will prove a good investment. What if we can't be sure our house will even be there in thirty years? Xanadu homes built in 1979 and 1980 had to be torn down by the early 1990s, they had begun to crumble so badly.

So if you want to express your architectural fantasies in a house that will turn into a major recycling problem in fifteen years, foam's for you.

FUNERAL ARRANGEMENTS
OF DUBIOUS TASTE

In 1903, a patent was issued for a novel method of preserving the dead. The corpse was to be posed in a naturalistic manner, coated with water glass (sodium silicate), and then sealed in a cube of molten glass. It was claimed that this process would prevent decomposition and allow for leisurely contemplation of the deceased.

In 1965, a U.S. patent (#3,188,712) was issued for the Vertical Casket. The bullet-shaped aluminum container had a ring at the tip through which a rope could be inserted to lower it into the ground. Intended as a space-saver, five vertical caskets could occupy the area required by one conventional type.

In 1974, Donald Wells patented a tombstone complete with a recording of the deceased, a projector to show scenes from his life, and a twenty-foot scroll for biographical data.

In 1978, Cliff Malbon of Daytona, Florida, received a patent for an inflatable vinyl coffin.

In 1980, Sid Goldstein, a New York City entrepreneur, proposed flying human ashes to the troposphere, then releasing them into the jet stream. Goldstein's first idea, rejected by NASA, was to inter human ashes on the moon. "The jet stream idea is better. This way, you've got the altitude, plus you can pass over your home and loved ones every twenty hours."

In 1986, A Florida company, Celestis Group, Inc., advertised that it would pack cremated remains into a gold-plated, lipstick-sized capsule; engrave it with the deceased's name, social security number and a religious symbol; and then launch it into space in a rocket payloader packed with fellow travelers. Rockets would be supplied by Space Services of Houston, Texas, a private company set up to launch commercial payloads. For $3,900 the payload would be put into orbit around the Earth, and for an additional $500 it would be sent into deep space. The orbiting mausoleum would feature a bright, reflective surface so that relatives might be able to remark on its passing. Celestis estimated that if it attracted 3% to 4% of those choosing cremation, the company would be commercially successful.

Vertical Casket. Patent No. 3,188,712—1965

A 1988 patent was issued for the cremation of corpses by solar power. A large bowl-shaped mirror would be constructed beside the funeral home. At the end of the service, the coffin would be dramatically lifted through a hole in the ceiling of the chapel by gantry and placed within the mirror at the focal point of the sun's rays, which would incinerate it. Kenneth Gardner, its inventor, felt that his system would eliminate the unfortunate connotation with hell fire suggested by sliding a coffin into an oven. He also felt that his system would realize man's dream to be reunited with the sun, the ultimate source of life. The system would have a backup flame broiler in case of cloudy weather or a backlog of funerals.

In 1993, Al Carpenter, a mortician in Alameda, California, introduced a do-it-yourself coffin for $9.95 that can also be used as a bookcase, chest, or coffee table.

GOLDFISH SWALLOWING AND ITS IMITATORS

In April, 1939, John Patrick, a student at the University of Chicago, received national attention for eating phonograph records. According to the Herald Tribune he had munched on several 78 r.p.m. records in front of a group of admiring coeds. "Fellow students," said Mr. Patrick, "I did this for my alma mater." No ill effects were reported.

Mr. Patrick's stunt was not imitated by legions of admirers. There are few rules in the world of fads, but one laid down by Ken ("Dr. Fad") Hakuta is this: "Don't invest in a sequel. There may be a *Beverly Hills Cop II* but there won't be a *Pet Sand*." The nature of a fad is that once it runs its course it becomes instantly passé and people look for something new and completely different. A fad is a joke that's not funny the second time around.

Mr. Patrick's stunt was performed on the heels of one of the great fad sensations of all time, the one that said it all about those madcap college kids—goldfish swallowing. That one began when Lothrop Withington, Jr. agreed to swallow a live three-inch goldfish in front of a crowd at the Harvard Union to win a $10 bet. (Actually, this was a stunt Mr. Withington had performed several times since his childhood, when he had seen it done by a Hawaiian.) Word leaked out to the press, and the March 3, 1939 event was covered by the *Boston Globe*. He was described as picking the fish out of a bowl, tilting his head back and dropping it down his throat. "Waves of perplexity passed over Withington's face once the fish had disappeared. There seemed to be some difficulty at first—some internal struggle—but after a brief moment of confusion the fish eater swallowed and all was well." He then drank several cupfuls of water from the fishbowl, pronouncing it "just like chowder." He then took out a toothbrush and cleaned his teeth (with a name like Lothrop Withington, Jr. you'd expect him to) and collected his bet.

When a Franklin and Marshall student swallowed three fish and claimed to have put Harvard in its place, another Harvard student swallowed 24 goldfish in five minutes, followed by an orange juice chaser. Then the battle was on between different colleges to see which could set the record. When a freshman at Kutztown State Teachers College put down forty-three in fifty-four minutes he was given an immediate suspension by the college president for "conduct unbecoming a student in a professional course." The animal protection groups began to get into the act as well. "No one knows how a fish feels," said Robert Sellar of the Boston Animal Rescue League. "We can't sidestep this issue." Doctors warned of intestinal parasites and other health risks to goldfish eaters. Nevertheless, the students swallowed away, and a St. Mary's University sophomore set the record of 210.

The goldfish craze had waned a month later when Mr. Patrick ate his records. Another student, this one at Lafayette, ate an entire magazine. Reports surfaced of other would-be trendsetters chowing down angleworms, beetles, gunpowder and—for the carnival geek effect—live white mice.

In a burst of nostalgia, goldfish swallowing made a brief comeback in 1967 at St. Joseph's College in Philadelphia, when one student swallowed 199.

Another attempt to bring glory to Mother Harvard occurred in 1973, when a small number of students began eating the university's light bulbs. The bulbs were broken up, then carefully chewed one shard at a time to a fine powder. Salad dressing was sometimes added to help it go down. Asked about their preferences in brands and wattages, one student expressed his confidence in the university's judgment, saying, "I eat whatever the university uses."

For some reason, there was no rash of imitators.

GRAVITY RESEARCH FOUNDATION

A lot has been written about the slow progress in cancer research and the lack of a breakthrough in fusion reaction, but little about the disappointing results of gravity research.

In 1948, awash in capital from his success on the stock market, Roger Babson funded the search for a "gravity screen," a substance which would effectively block the force of gravity the way a window shade blocks light. Babson was personally aquainted with Thomas Edison, who had once remarked to him, "You've got to find something that isolates from gravity. I think it's coming about from some sort of alloy." Armed with this valuable lead, Babson set up the Gravity Research Foundation in a large brick building in New Boston, New Hampshire, and began collecting information. Since Edison experimented with 8,000 materials before he hit on the right filament for the electric light, Babson figured that a similar search might unearth the desired gravity screen. Such an alloy would have numerous practical applications, such as in flying carpets and perpetual motion machines. Babson had no formal training in science, though it is rumored he studied the Flash Gordon comic strip on a daily basis. The foundation sponsors an annual essay contest and collects scientific research on the subject of gravity.

GREENIE BEANIE

In the early sixties, an ad appeared for an exciting new concept in headgear. We see the Kingston Trio—at that time, a top folk group—strumming their instruments as a few coeds stand by admiringly. On their heads, each is wearing what looks like the oversized suction cup from a plunger, from the middle of which sprouts a tuft of... something. The copy explains:

"Have a bash with a GREENIE BEANIE! From coast to coast, everywhere the young set is going wild for the hat with the green "hair"... the fabulous GREENIE BEANIE. On campuses, at the beaches, at football games... wherever there are young moderns, there are GREENIE BEANIES. And what a sensation the GREENIE BEANIE is. It's a hat complete with green "hair" growing out of the top... real, live green grass you can trim into a "butch," a "mohawk," a "flip," or a "bob," or let grow long and groovey. Built into the top of every GREENIE BEANIE is a chemically-treated tray of lawn seed. You just water regularly and in five days or less you'll have a real lawn growing out the top. And with each one you receive FREE a special watering measure and "Keep off the grass" sign."

The GREENIE BEANIE was available by mail order for $1.59, two for $3.00.

GROCERY CONCEPTS THAT DIDN'T MAKE IT

- What with Pop Tarts and Eggo waffles, the toaster seems to be to breakfast what the microwave is to dinner. Efforts to extend its versatility have not always been successful. Downyflake Toaster Eggs made a brief appearance, but were not rated Grade A by consumers. Had they been, they might have been served with ReddiWip's Reddi Bacon, foil-wrapped, pre-cooked slices of bacon you dropped into the toaster. Keep the fire extinguisher handy, though—leaking bacon fat set some toasters ablaze.
- The incendiary problem also plagued Toaster

Chicken Patties, a toaster-ready meat entree. Ditto for The Electric French Fry, a slab of fries that were supposed to be popped in the toaster to heat, and then broken apart to serve. They looked like a picket fence and tasted like one too.

- Nestea's Tea Whiz. If you were marketing a yellowish, carbonated, lemon-flavored drink, isn't that the last thing you'd call it?
- The Gerber Products Company had a problem. Its consumers kept growing up and eating some other company's food. So in the 1970s Gerber came out with Singles, an attempt to market food to the growing numbers of American adults living alone. The offerings were gourmet, such as sweet-and-sour pork, beef burgundy, Mediterranean vegetables, and creamed beef, and came in baby-food jars. Problems? Two. The Gerber name and baby-food style jars were hard for adults to get past. Secondly, the name Singles suggested loneliness, reminding people that they were going through life as a party of one.
- Johnson, Inc., marketed a microwaveable hot mint fudge sundae. The hot fudge topping was supposed to warm up, the ice cream to stay cold. Who could believe it?
- Roland Rat, a canned pasta-and-sauce product from Britain's HP Foods, Ltd. Pasta designed in the shape of rats test-marketed very well in Great Britain, where 97 percent of kids surveyed said they'd like to eat rodent-shaped noodles. British humor does not always cross the Atlantic successfully.
- As part of La Choy's Fresh and Lite line of low-fat frozen Chinese entrees, Frozen Egg Rolls seemed like a natural. These weren't little appetizer-type egg rolls, but big meaty main courses. Trouble was, they took about a half hour to heat up (long enough to drive to your nearest Chinese restaurant from virtually anywhere in the continental United States), and by the time the filling was hot the

shell was soggy. They died along with the rest of the Fresh and Lite line, which consumers thought sounded too much like a feminine hygiene product.

- A poorly-packaged product made a brief, but memorable appearance in the early 1970s. A snack called HITS had its name spelled boldly out across its bag. When lined up end-to-end on supermarket shelves, the eye-catching display read "HITSHITSHITHITS." It was quickly pulled.

- Avert was "the virucidal tissue," chemically treated to kill your cold germs when you used them to blew your nose. A good idea, but unfortunately most people didn't know what virucidal means—it just sounds scary.

- How about Burns & Rickers freeze-dried vegetable crisps? Each bag contained a mixture of vegetables, including sweet potatoes, carrots, string beans, squash, zucchini and onions. Rated one of the worst new products in AcuPoll's consumer survey for 1994. Their considered analysis: "Blech!" Low marks also went to a new chocolate-flavored salsa.

- Colgate's Bite 'N Brush, a chewable toothpaste that came in tablet form. There were also scented toothbrushes, impreganted with the aroma of strawberry, chocolate, lemon lime, vanilla and orange-ice cream.

- Presto-Wine was put on the market by a Toronto firm in 1984. It was a purple powder containing yeast and flavoring; after sugar and water were added and it was left to sit for a month it turned into what purported to be wine. Could be useful to would-be messiahs.

GUITAR SUIT

"I can feel the vibrations in my body. I know what an expectant mother must feel like. I am the music," said Dan Hartman, bass guitartist with the Edgar Winter

Group, in 1974. The hyperbole was provoked by his Guitar Suit, a musical instrument that he designed and wore as clothing. The $5,000, silverized body-suit was custom-made from a rubbery fabric called stretch laurex. It featured a "pelvic pocket" into which he could plug the neck of his electric guitar. Electrical contacts inside the pocket were wired to a cigarette-pack-sized amplifier in a thigh pocket. Through an aerial sewn along his leg, it wired the music he played to the amplifiers back stage, which fed it to the bank of speakers. The suit was equipped with knobs on his left sleeve to control the tone and volume.

GUITAR SUIT

Hartman pointed out the several advantages of his Guitar Suit to *Time* magazine, which suggested it might revolutionize the look of a rock concert. It freed him from entangling electrical cords. It removed the danger of electrocution when playing outdoor gigs in inclement weather. Best of all was the contribution his stomach made to the quality of the sound. "The abdomen is the most resonant part of the body," he observed.

GYROCOPTER

"In spite of all the publicity talk about the 'jet age,' 90 percent of our people have never been off the ground. In fact, there are fewer privately-owned aircraft in the entire U.S. now than there are cars in Azusa, California," said Igor Bensen in 1964.

To free the masses from their earthly bonds, the

Russian-born engineer founded the Bensen Aircraft Corp. in Raleigh, North Carolina, in the 1950s. The vehicle of our deliverance was to be his Gyrocopter, a one-person, open-sided mini-helicopter—little more than a flying chair. It flew at 60 mph, and required no more open space than a tennis court in which to land. It could rise to an altitude of two miles, though most pilots preferred to stay under 600 feet. Its gas tank held six gallons, about enough for an hour's flight. It weighed 285 pounds and could carry a 250-pound payload. "You're all by yourself," a California banker and Gyrocopter pilot enthused. "The wind whirls by your ears, and you can often change direction by simply moving your body. You're really flying by the seat of your pants."

Bensen's vision of the future was "A Chopper in

Every Garage." Bensen founded the Popular Rotocraft Association (membership as of 1966: 4,000) and gave public demonstrations in order to drum up enthusiasm. He liked to run errands in his own copter, touching down in a parking lot, making a few adjustments for land travel, then zipping into traffic for stops at the bank, post office and grocery store. (In its roadable mode the Gyrocopter could do 50 mph.) He refueled at a gas station, then left the crawling lanes of traffic for the wide open spaces above.

The Federal Aviation Agency required all Gyrocopters to be at least 51 percent owner built in order to qualify as experimental aircraft, avoiding the complex certification procedures. The minimal parts and plans kit, without engine, sold for $700; a complete kit went for $2,600. There was supposed to be a deal with Montgomery Ward to sell Gyrocopters (or Convertabirds, as they were sometimes called) through its stores and catalogs. This would have brought the price down to $920 for a kit including a new 72-hp engine. According to Bensen, it was so simple "a teenager can build one and a grandmother can learn in a few hours to fly one." Flying it required only a student license.

Gyrocopter enthusiasts claimed that their craft was less dangerous than other aircraft; if its engine failed, it would "auto-rotate" slowly to Earth, settling gently at no more than ten miles per hour. Difficulties were experienced by those who had not followed directions when assembling their Gyrocopters. One handyman mounted his rotor upside down, started it up and remained firmly earthbound. Another added bolts to eliminate rotor teetering; when he took off, his seat began spinning around, he flipped over and crashed. Fortunately, the Gyrocopter was what pilots call "a forgiving plane." Its frame absorbed most of the shock of a crash, and it had little mass to crush or entangle the pilot. In its coverage of a Gyrocopter fly-in at the El Mirage dry lake in California, *Time* magazine described a crash which totalled a copter, but left its pilot without a scratch.

Gyrocopter-type craft are still available in kit form, but Bensen's vision of one in every garage did not come to pass.

GYROJET PISTOL

"You can't say civilization don't advance," observed Will Rogers, "in every war they kill you a new way."

Actually, that's not true. The basic design of the cartridge fired in hand-held weapons has remained unchanged since about 1873. A brass casing is filled with gunpowder, topped with a bullet and detonated by a primer in its base. Ingenuity marches on, though, and from time to time attempts are made to change this settled arrangement. In 1960 Robert Mainhardt, president of MBAssociates of San Ramon, California, engineer and boyhood model rocketry enthusiast, introduced the Gyrojet pistol. It was basically a hand-held launcher for a miniature ballistic missile. The missile was 13 mm. (about a half inch) in diameter and gyroscopically stabilized by canted ports in its base. Burnout time was 0.12 seconds and burnout velocity was 1250 feet per second, about as fast as a 9 mm. bullet. The design offered certain unique advantages. It was nearly silent and produced no recoil. The gun itself was extremely simple and reliable, and needed no oiling or cleaning. The entire round was fired out of the barrel, eliminating problems of ejection and jamming. It delivered twice the punch of a .45 caliber bullet. It could be fired underwater.

For six years the company tried unsuccessfully to persuade the U.S. Army to adopt the Gyrojet as its issue sidearm, even producing a twelve-barreled model that Mainhardt touted as "Just the thing to wipe out a nest of Vietcong with one squeeze of the trigger." In order to finance continued development, it then went to the civilian market, offering the Mark I Presentation Model Gyrojet for $250.00. According to the catalogue, "Each pistol is engraved and serially numbered, mounted in an attractive walnut case with 10 dummy rockets and a bronze medal honoring rocket pioneer Robert H. Goddard." Reportedly, two Soviet military attachés traveled to California to buy one, but were turned away at the gun shop.

Mainhardt continued to develop his idea, even coming up with miniature Finjet missiles that could be fired from inside cigarettes, for the well-equipped CIA operative. "The filter tip would block the exhaust," he maintained, "but if he puts the wrong end in his mouth it will cure him of smoking for good."

The Gyrojet's offbeat, state-of-the-art quality caused it to be featured in the 1967 James Bond feature *You Only*

Live Twice, in which space-age ninjas train with it, blowing large, flaming holes in man-sized silhouette targets. James Bond uses the cigarette gag, of course. Such glamorous showcasing should have done for the Gyrojet what the *Dirty Harry* did for Smith & Wesson's previously obscure .44 magnum— blown its sales through the roof. The Gyrojet had problems, though, that ensured its failure. The rockets required 15 yards to reach full power; at normal handgun range the rocket was alarmingly feeble. It was extremely inaccurate, spreading its shots 15 inches or more at 25 yards. Its rocket was fiercely incendiary— great for the movies but not too cool for outdoor practice. Finally, there is the matter of cost. The ammunition went for about $1.50 *a round* at a time when $50 would supply a surplus 9mm. with 100 rounds of ammunition, putting it out of the range of anyone whose defense budget fell much short of the U.S. government's. The gun was discontinued in 1969.

HAIR CLOTHING

In 1969, according to *Esquire*, a New York designer displayed a line of women's fashions incorporating human hair. His concepts included a pants suit trimmed with straight white hair; a vest and skirt made from curly black hair; a long, formal, hair dress; and a coat made from brown hair. There was also a hair bikini, hair neckties and hair boots, and a promise from the designer that hair hats would be forthcoming. And surely hair shirts for those repenting their wretched excess.

"HAPPY TO BE ME" DOLL

Noting that, for many of her women friends, "bad feelings about their weight overshadowed the many things they had to be proud of," Cathy Meredig, a thirty-eight-year old software designer, resolved to do something about the problem. She believed that children formed their ideas about body image as early as age three, and that the dolls they were given created unrealistic expectations; who but Barbie has proportions of 36-30-32? Meredig designed an alternative, "Happy to Be Me." The doll came in at a more realistic 36-27-38, with non-elongated neck and legs, and feet that were not permanently stuck in the high-heel position.

Manufacturers were not taken with the idea, claiming that "American women wouldn't get it," so in 1991 Meredig took $100,000 of her own money and found-ed High Self-Esteem Toys to market it. Despite favorable press attention, stores were not interested, find-ing it "too education-al." That's not consid-ered praise in the toy business.

Actually, the toy manufacturers and mer-chants understood one of those cruel truths that there's just no getting around. Barbie hasn't clobbered the competition for decades by accident. Behind that perky smile is a battle-hardened veteran of the doll wars whose motto is "Mess With the Best, Die Like the Rest."

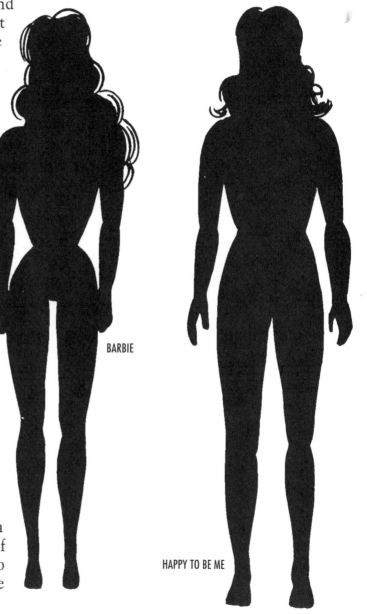

BARBIE

HAPPY TO BE ME

HATS FROM HELL

- A Mr. R. F. S. Heath received U.S. Patent #273,074 in 1883 for his idea of luminous hats. A hat, cap, or bonnet could be dipped or coated in a luminous (and yes, carcinogenic) material such as radium, that would make it beautiful at night and much easier to find in dark closets. As a safety feature, it would also help to keep tabs on anyone who might be involved in a hazardous activity at night.
- No inventive mind could look at a top hat and not

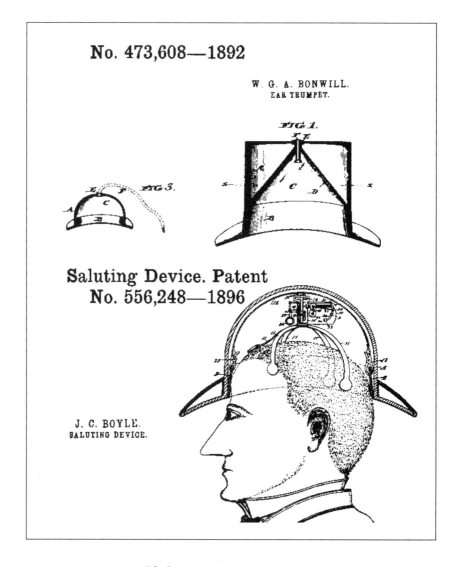

No. 473,608—1892

W. G. A. BONWILL.
EAR TRUMPET.

FIG. 1.

FIG. 3.

Saluting Device. Patent
No. 556,248—1896

J. C. BOYLE.
SALUTING DEVICE.

be inspired to take advantage of all that wasted space. In 1892 W. G. A. Bonwill received U.S. Patent #473,608 for his Ear Trumpet Hat for the hard of hearing. The top hat contains a funnel which culminates in a hole at the center of the crown. The wearer removes his hat and points the bottom at the source of the sound he wants amplified while holding the end of the funnel to his ear.

• In a previous era, when manners were more conscientiously observed and hats routinely worn, special challenges arose. How was a gentleman to tip his hat if his arms were full of packages? James C. Boyle addressed the problem in 1896 with his Saluting Device (U.S. Patent # 556, 248). A wind-up device was attached to the hat. At its base are a number of curved-spring fingers which hold it to the gentleman's head. All he need now do is bow his head slightly and a pendulum triggers machinery which lifts the hat, turns it 360 degrees, and settles it back in place. And you thought those Victorians didn't know how to have a good time.

• The Hat Guard. Hats are removed indoors and hung on hatracks, and thus can easily be purloined. U.S. Patent #1,098,691 was issued in 1914 for a device that delivers a pointed message to the hat-

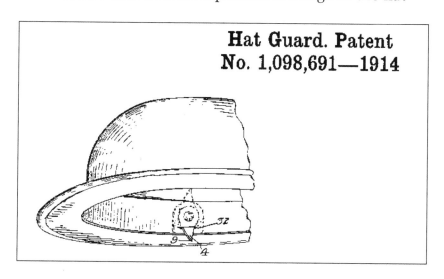

Hat Guard. Patent No. 1,098,691—1914

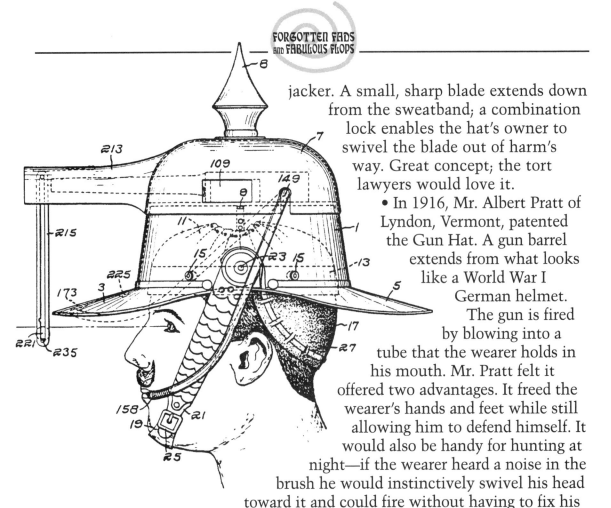

jacker. A small, sharp blade extends down from the sweatband; a combination lock enables the hat's owner to swivel the blade out of harm's way. Great concept; the tort lawyers would love it.

- In 1916, Mr. Albert Pratt of Lyndon, Vermont, patented the Gun Hat. A gun barrel extends from what looks like a World War I German helmet. The gun is fired by blowing into a tube that the wearer holds in his mouth. Mr. Pratt felt it offered two advantages. It freed the wearer's hands and feet while still allowing him to defend himself. It would also be handy for hunting at night—if the wearer heard a noise in the brush he would instinctively swivel his head toward it and could fire without having to fix his sights on the target. Then again, it could also produce interesting results if the wearer sneezed, belched or let loose a heartfelt sigh.

- Try this on for size—a hard, plastic, beanie with a swivelling arm on top to which a long, flexible streamer is attached. Fasten the chin strap and swing your head in circles. You can make the streamer whirl in pretty patterns. You could also give yourself a terrific headache and poke your eye out. This 1966 novelty item is from that museum of forlorn fads.

- The Cooling Unit for a Hat was patented in 1967 (#3,353,191). A solar cell on top of the hat powered a fan within the hat's crown. The fan could be slowed down, or shut off entirely, by positioning a sliding cover over the solar unit. Air was admitted

Cooling Unit for a Hat. Patent No. 3,353,191—1967

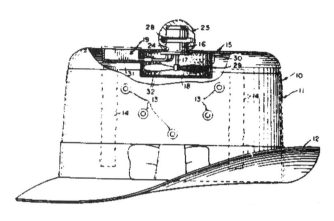

through vent holes in the side of the hat. A wind-up version of this idea was patented in 1860.

- The Carry-All Hat, (U.S. Patent 3,496,575) was a woman's pillbox-style hat with a compartment where cosmetics, keys, money or jewelry might be stored. For security it featured a chin strap.

- The Alarm Cap. A device to keep drivers from falling asleep at the wheel, this ball cap contained a 'tilt' mechanism which sounded an alarm if the driver's head began to nod excessively.

- In 1979, Japanese scientists invented an "electronic head cooler," which, according to Family Safety magazine, refrigerates the brow when wrapped around a driver's forehead and plugged into the car's cigarette lighter. Wider acceptance of this item might have cut down on L.A. freeway shootings.

- The Smoker's Hat was patented in 1989 (U.S. Patent 4,858,627). A helmet-like apparatus that enables the smoker to pursue his vice in public without fouling the environment. The visor contains an intake which pumps in the exhaled smoke, then processes it through a system which purifies, deionizes, and deodorizes it before releasing it. The hat also features a holder for a lit cigarette, a pouch for a cigarette pack and an integral ashtray. The hat seemed designed to add further humiliation to this supremely stigmatized habit.

• 1990 saw the introduction of designer yarmulkes. The yarmulkes were decorated with Ninja Turtles, sports gear, dinosaurs, baseball emblem and sports gear. Oy gevalt!

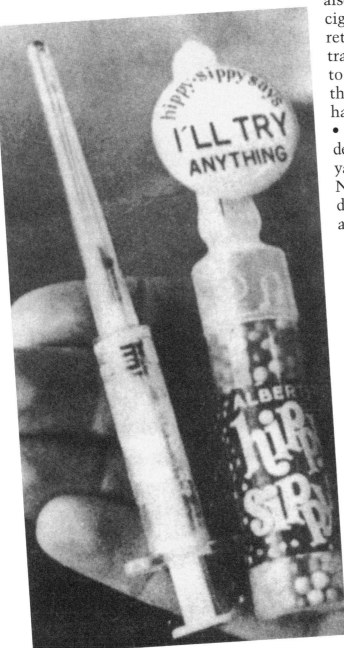

HIPPY-SIPPY

Offered in festive 1968 by the Alberts company, Hippy-Sippy consisted of multi-colored pill-sized candies sold in a toy hypodermic needle. In case the drug analogy escaped anyone, it came with buttons carrying messages such as: "Hippy-Sippy says: I'll try anything," and "Happiness Lives." The candy, which definitely gives new meaning to the term "junk food," was singled out for criticism in toy-critic Edward Swartz's *Toys That Don't Care.*

HI-RISE CAMPING

Now that we are accustomed to people going "camping" in mobile homes with VCRs and microwave ovens, what's the next step? Evidently it wasn't Hi-Rise Camping.

In the 1970s, Wesley Hurley noticed that most people don't want to sacrifice their modern conveniences to go camping. When you go to the wilderness you risk bugs, poison ivy, and the alarming remoteness of all-nite delis and drug stores. So he planned to construct the world's first hi-rise campground in downtown New Orleans, for a projected cost of $4 million. The building would be twenty-stories high, with parking on the eight lower floors. The camper could then take the elevator to one of the the upper floors, which would contain 240 individual campsites. Intrepid backpackers might take the stairs. Each site would be covered in astroturf and equipped with electrical connections. Piped-in owl and cricket sounds to mask traffic noises would have been a nice touch.

"It is designed for today's different brand of camping," Hurley proclaimed. "People don't want the woodsy bit now; they want to camp in comfort near the city."

"I"

In 1969, the avant-garde writer Juan Luis Castillejo published a book of several hundred pages printed randomly with the letter "i." It was intended as an attack against "the tyranny of words we call literature." With sales unencouraging, Castillejo dropped plans to have it translated for foreign markets.

I HATE PEAS

In the early 1970s Frank Aldridge got the idea for "I Hate Peas." At the dinner table with his 5-year-old son, he noticed that "he ate his hamburger, he ate his potatoes, but he spread his peas all over the plate." When asked why, the boy answered, "Daddy, I hate peas."

In an instant, Mr. Aldridge was certain he had a sure-fire product. As president of American Kitchen Foods, a french-fry producer in Maine, he knew just what to do. To make peas appetizing to picky kids he mushed them up and extruded them in the shape of french-fried potatoes. The come-on: "If your family hates peas but loves crisp french fries, try I Hate Peas. The new way to vegetable goodness." Soon he was shipping I Hate Peas to supermarkets all over the U.S., along with I Hate Spinach, I Hate Beets, and other wholesome vegetables in disguise. Mothers loved it—it jumped off the shelves. But kids didn't fall for the reverse psychology. The knew that a pea by any other name tastes the same.

Mr. Aldridge discontinued the product line, sold the company, and now runs a restaurant chain in Atlanta.

ICEBERG AIRCRAFT CARRIERS

German U-Boats took a terrible toll on Allied shipping in the early years of World War II, sinking thousands of vessels. Air cover was the best protection against the submarines, but flying range was limited to a few hundred miles off the American and English coasts. In 1942 Geoffrey Pyke, an inventor attached to the British War Office, proposed a solution to this problem.

First a word about Geoffrey Pyke, a classic English eccentric who had become a minor hero for his unofficial exploits in World War I. He had slipped into Berlin, planning to send back reports to the London *Daily Chronicle*, but was soon captured and told he would be shot as a spy. Upon investigation, though, the Germans realized he was more Inspector Clouseau than James Bond, and put him in a POW camp. Every day, guards would check the buildings in the camp before the prisoners were locked in their barracks. Pyke noticed that the sun always shone directly into the guard's eyes as he checked a certain shed, and reasoned that if he hid in there he would not be seen and thus could make his escape. Indeed he did, and back in England

he gave a series of lectures recounting his adventures. One such address was given at Wellington, his former boarding school, where he told the assembly that even during his darkest hours, when he was sure he would be executed by a firing squad, he was never quite so unhappy as he was when he had been a student there.

At the time of the Spanish Civil War, Pyke devoted his inventive energies toward trying to develop equipment for the Loyalist side. He designed special sidecars for Harley-Davidson motorcycles that made them into mini-ambulances. He also suggested using pedal power to shunt trains in railroad yards. As World War II loomed, Pyke hoped to prevent it by presenting Hitler with an opinion poll indicating that his people did not want war. The polling data would be secretly gathered by intrepid English students who would travel through Germany disguised as golfers. The preliminary data looked promising, but when Hitler invaded Poland, Pyke's golfing-agents barely escaped with their lives.

Pyke's inventiveness was tapped by Admiral Mountbatten, chief of Combined Operations, who took him on his staff as part of a group of brainstorming scientists and original thinkers. One of his original notions was for mechanized sleds that British commandos could use to attack German installations in occupied Norway. At first he thought the vehicle would need a crew of three, with one to guard it while the other two performed their sabotage. Then he decided that he could dispense with the guard if it were labeled with signs in German, reading: "Officer's Latrine. For Colonels Only." No German soldier would dare enter a vehicle so marked, he reasoned. The scheme was approved, but the vehicles were developed too late to be of use in the war.

Pyke was a fountain of ideas, but his most audacious proposal addressed the problem of air-cover for Allied shipping. His solution: giant, man-made icebergs that could be used as mid-Atlantic airfields. They were to be 300 feet wide and 2,000 feet long, displacing 1,800,000 tons of water—26 times the displacement of the ocean liner Queen Elizabeth. Beneath the landing deck, inside 50-foot-thick walls, would be crew quarters, hangers, electric engines for power and a gigantic refrigeration plant to keep the whole thing intact. For defense, the vessel could spray enemy ships with super-cooled water which would encase them in ice. The project was code-named *Habbakuk*, after a minor prophet in the Old Testament who says: "I am doing a work in your days which you would not believe if told." Needless to say, these behemoths would have been impervious to torpedoes, though it hasn't been recorded whether the danger from rock salt was considered. Pyke even suggested using the vessels to attack ports. Their water cannons could seal off railway tunnels, and they could unload blocks of ice and build a floating wall around the harbor entrance. Pyke even had visions of sealing Hitler alive in his bunker.

To build these floating airfields Pyke developed "Pykrete", a mixture of 10% wood pulp and 90% water. When frozen it was claimed to have special properties: it could be sawed and hammered like wood, was as strong as concrete, and amazingly slow to melt. Mountbatten was so taken with the stuff that he rushed into Winston Churchill's private quarters, found him in the tub, and promptly dropped a block of Pykrete into the bath water to demonstrate its remarkable properties. Churchill was convinced. Later, to demonstrate the material's toughness before the allied chiefs of staff, Mountbatten took out his revolver and fired at a chunk of the stuff. The ricocheting bullet just missed the assembled chiefs, lending additional impact to the presentation.

Operation Habbukak forged ahead. A scaled-down prototype was built on Patricia Lake in Alberta, Canada, under a dummy boathouse to maintain secrecy. It lasted through a hot summer with no sign of melting.

The Normandy landings made further development of the iceberg aircraft carrier unnecessary. It also had been calculated that building a single bergship would take 8,000 men eight months of work in arctic conditions, and would cost at least $70 million.

INCHON

In the 1970s, the Korean evangelist Reverend Moon was causing considerable concern. He was accused of brainwashing legions of young people into joining his Unification Church, who then peddled flowers on the street to raise money for him, or worked for low wages in his businesses and industries. He owned a large arms factory in South Korea, and had ties to the Korean CIA. He set up *Insight* magazine and newspapers such as the *Washington Times* to reflect his conservative political views, and contributed to political causes. The Divine Principle that he propounded implied that he, Reverend Moon, was the reincarnation of Christ. Many wondered what Moon, with his enormous wealth, army of devoted followers, political connections and messianic vision, really wanted. In 1982, we found out. He wanted to make

a movie. The movie he made was *Inchon*. The *Guinness Book of Records* lists it as the biggest flop of all time.

The story behind this epic catastrophe begins eight years earlier. Those flower vendors were bringing in an estimated $26 million a year, not to mention the profits in the arms business, so the Reverend had a surplus of cash. He decided to use some of it to set up a film production company, One Way Productions. He put a long-time disciple and business associate in charge of the operation, Japanese newspaper publisher Mitsuharu Ishii, who had no prior experience in the film industry. The first thought was to make a film about the life of Christ, but that was humbly put aside for later. If not the King of Kings, why not the King himself? Ishii met several times with Elvis in Memphis to discuss a project. Unfortunately, Elvis died before a deal could be consummated, so we'll never know if Elvis could have made a movie worse than *Blue Hawaii*. Finally the decision was reached. Ishii would make a military epic about General Douglas MacArthur, one that would not only celebrate the bond between Korea and the United States, but would enable Moon to really stick it to the North Korean communists.

The decision made, he began hiring the best talent that money could buy, a fairly non-exclusive category in Hollywood. Robin Moore, whose right-wing credentials had been established with *The Green Berets* and *The French Connection* (and somewhat tarnished with *The Happy Hooker*) signed on as scriptwriter. Sir Laurence Olivier was available for $1.25 million. Jaqueline Bisset, whose wet T-shirt made *The Deep* a hit, commanded an astonishing $1.65 million—$825,000 per breast, as critic Michael Medved pointed out. Others who lined their pockets included Toshiro Mifune (to pull in the Japanese), Ben Gazzara, Richard Roundtree (for *Shaft* fans), David Janssen, and Rex Reed (possibly a vain attempt to buy off the critical clique).

The title was to be *Oh, Inchon!*, which struck Moon as masterfully evocative of the opening verse of the *Star-Spangled Banner*. The story revolved around MacArthur's surprise landing at Inchon Harbor in 1950, an attempt to cut off the Communist forces that ultimately brought the Chinese into the conflict and helped cost him his commission. There was lots of divine intervention, of the sort that Reverend Moon claimed to benefit from regularly, though apparently not in this particular enterprise. North Koreans were portrayed as sub-human, demonic forces; there was not a single speaking part for the enemy.

Problems plagued *Oh, Inchon!* from the outset. Production was to begin in Korea in January, 1979. The government was in the midst of delicate negotiations with its northern antagonists and did not want to raise tensions, and so withheld necessary permits. As week after week dragged by, with the assembled cast and crew drawing $200,000 a day, the only progress that was made was the decision to drop the *Oh* from the movie's title, and go with a bold, solitary *Inchon!* When the government finally relented, Nature kicked in. Typhoons destroyed an elaborate set and earth-quake-driven tides swept away a fourteen-ton camera crane. Heavy rains mired the tanks in mud. The mounting expenses did not seem to trouble the folks at One Way Productions. Money for cast and crew was handed out from cash-stuffed suitcases.

A stickler for authenticity, Moon insisted that one climactic scene involving 300 ships be filmed in Inchon Harbor, despite the tricky tides that had bedeviled MacArthur himself. Director Terence Young spent days overcoming the logistics of the operation. His instructions called for the armada to steam into the harbor in perfect formation, then take an abrupt turn to the left to provide a visually-dramatic shot. With all the ships assembled, after waiting hours for the perfect light, the sequence commenced. With the cameras all prepared to film the left turn, the ships turned right instead. The mistake was traced to a Korean assistant director, whose walkie-talkie was broken but who had declined to mention it for fear of losing face. Of course there can be no price put on a man's dignity, but in this case it came in at approximately a half million dollars. Other snafus were even more expensive. The final sequence, in which MacArthur delivers the Lord's Prayer to an assembled multitude, was redone several times until it met with Moon's satisfaction. Though the three-minute scene itself is unspectacular, the cost of the post-production shooting was. It entailed reassembling the entire cast in Korea at a cost of nearly $1 million, and later flying Olivier to Dublin for further reshoots.

The principal photography had so far come to $26 million, but the lengthy postproduction efforts added a staggering $22 million to the tally, making *Inchon* at $48 million the most expensive film up to that time. (Movie costs are hard to pin down, and *Guinness* has arrived at a different figure than the one generally accepted—a mind-boggling $102 million!)

Unfortunately, money alone cannot buy high production values, and the film contained more than its share of gaffes. In one battle scene, bodies fly in the air before shells burst, rather than after. Roundtree's character is blown up in his jeep, only to return moments later, none the worse for wear. MacArthur's trousers change color twice during a long speech—from beige to dark green and then back again.

The association with the controversial cult leader, along with the fact that *Inchon* was a bigger bomb than any dropped during the Korean War, made distributors reluctant to handle the film. MGM/UA finally accepted the bomb disposal chores, for a deal that reportedly included an up-front cash payoff. They did insist that the exclamation point be dropped from the title, and that Moon's credit (above that of director, producer or star) be

LAWRENCE OLIVIER AS GENERAL MACARTHUR TOASTS *INCHON* PRODUCER MITSUHARU ISHII.

changed from "*Spiritual* Advisor" to "*Special* Advisor."

As to the critical reception, it could best be described as enthusiastically unkind. The title of "the worst movie ever made" was bestowed by several reviewers. Many gave Olivier the benefit of the doubt, inferring that his atrocious performance was his droll way of distancing himself from the project. Seeking advice from General Alexander Haig, who had served with MacArthur, Olivier had learned that the great man's speech pattern was almost identical to that of W.C. Fields, and played it that way. Vincent Canby noted that "When he catches a glimpse of a bust of Julius Caesar in his office, he does the sort of flinch affected by W. C. Fields on colliding with a small, disgusting child." Of course, it must have been hard to play it straight in scenes such as the one where he's leaving for the office and tells his wife, "I shall return—but not too late for dinner." A further handicap was his heavy make-up. The wig, putty nose, chin, and mascara took four hours to apply everyday and made him look appropriately, according to the *Village Voice*, like "a broken-down tart."

Shocked by this horrendous reception, Moon did his best to save his investment. He took out full-page newspaper ads, imploring the public to ignore the critics and see his film. He sponsored "The *Inchon* Million Dollar Sweepstakes," with prizes for movie-goers ranging from a brand new Rolls Royce Corniche down to "50,000 beautifully illustrated *Inchon* souvenir books." (With the low turn-out, your odds would have to be pretty good on that Rolls.) His glassy-eyed moonies passed out leaflets in front of the theaters, begging passersby to enter. Unfortunately, this only strengthened the association of the film with the reviled Reverend. Many potential viewers were afraid that if they signed up for a sweepstakes or attended the movie, the next thing they knew they might wake up at one of those camps in upstate New York, surrounded by smiling faces singing "When the Red, Red Robin Goes Bob-Bob-Bobbin' Along."

Inchon made a reported $1.9 million. One Way

Productions expressed its confidence that the film would eventually make money. It also claimed to have a multipart series on the Bible in the works, for which $1 billion had been budgeted. But they've got to sell a lot of guns and roses first.

THE IND COLD CURE

In 1981 Norman Lake, an engineer from Lancaster, Pennsylvania, said he might have discovered a cure for the common cold. Lake unveiled the Inductive Nasal Device, which looks like a pair of miniature earmuffs—two white plastic knobs at each end of a U-shaped piece of piano wire. Lake said that the treatment required the cold sufferer to clamp the IND on the nose for fifteen to thirty minutes a day until symptoms disappeared. If you kept it up for a week to ten days, it would probably do the trick.

INSECT FOOD

In the early 1960s, Reese Finer Foods offered the following canned insect foods as part of its gourmet food line:
- Chocolate Covered South American Giant Ants
- Chocolate Covered Bees
- Chocolate Covered Caterpillars
- Chocolate Coated Menagerie
  (Ants, Bees, Caterpillars, and Grasshoppers)
- French Fried South American Giant Ants
- French Fried Grasshoppers
- French Fried Silkworms
- Roasted Caterpillars

The insect foods even had cost-cutting competitors. Morris Kushner, who conceived the gourmet line for Reese, accused rivals of selling ordinary house ants dipped in chocolate. Reese used only the finest Colombian big-bottomed ants, big as bees.

Mr. Kushner was once a guest on *You Bet Your Life*.

Groucho Marx, the show's host, told him, "I can't eat your chocolate-covered ants. The chocolate upsets my stomach."

Other foods once considered exotic, such as chives, artichoke hearts, and macadamia nuts, survived to become staples. Insects, unfortunately, did not make the cut, and their sales were discontinued in America in the early 1970s.

Most Americans would eat a beetle grub only after first anesthetizing themselves with the tequila it was

THE FOOD INSECTS
NEWSLETTER

NOVEMBER, 1994   VOLUME VII, NO. 3

Some Insect Foods of the American Indians: And How the Early Whites Reacted to Them

There is a small fly (*Hydropyrus hians*), belonging to the group known as "shore flies" (Diptera; Ephydridae), that formerly bred in vast numbers in the alkaline waters of Mono Lake and other alkaline lakes in the California-Nevada border region. It was called *kutsavi* (or variations thereof) by the Paiute and other tribes. The fly pupae washed ashore in long windrows. J. Ross Browne[1], who visited Mono Lake in about 1865, told of encountering a deposit of pupae about two feet deep and three or four feet wide that extended "like a vast rim" around the lake:

"I saw no end to it during a walk of several miles along the beach . . . It would appear that the worms [read fly pupae], as soon as they attain locomotion, creep up from the water, or are deposited on the beach by the waves during some of those violent gales which prevail in this region. The Mono Indians derive from them a fruitful source of subsistence. By drying them in the sun and mixing them with acorns, berries, grass-seeds, and other articles of food gathered up in the mountains, they make a conglomerate called *cuchaba*, which they use as a kind of bread. I am told it is very nutritious and not at all unpalatable. The worms are also eaten in their natural condition. . . . [It is] considered a delicacy to fry them. . . . When prepared by a skillful cook they . . . [I was not] hungry enough to require one . . . but would recommend any friend . . . [to buy] a pound or two and let me know the . . . [con]venience. . . . There must be hundreds, perhaps . . . of these oleaginous insects cast up on the beach . . . no longer of starvation on the shores of Mono. The Indian . . . [if] snowed in, flooded out, or cut off by aboriginal hordes, but . . . can always rely upon the beach for fat-meat."

William Brewer[2], a professor of agriculture, had sampled *kutsavi* during a visit to Mono Lake in 1863. Noting that hundreds of bushels could be collected, he wrote:

"The Indians come far and near to gather them. The worms are dried in the sun, the shell rubbed off, when a yellowish kernal remains, like a small yellow grain of rice. This is oily, very nutritious, and not unpleasant to the taste, and under the name of *koo-chah-bee* forms a very important article of food. The Indians gave me some; it does not taste bad, and if one were ignorant of its origin, it would make fine soup. Gulls, ducks, snipe, frogs, and Indians fatten on it."

Somewhat earlier, in 1845, Captain John C. Fremont[3] was impressed with a windrow of *kutsavi* which he described as 10-20 feet in breadth and 7-12 inches deep. Fremont related an experience told to

him by an old hunter, Mr. Joseph Walker. Walker and his men had surprised a party of several Indian families encamped near a small lake who had abandoned their lodges at his approach, leaving everything behind them:

"Being in a starving condition, they were delighted to find in the abandoned lodges a number of skin bags, containing a quantity of what appeared to be fish, dried and pounded. On this they made a hearty supper; and were gathering around an abundant breakfast the next morning, when Mr. Walker discovered that it was . . . of worms, or a similar worm, that the bags had been filled. The stom[achs] of the stout trappers were not proof against their prejudices, and the . . . sive food was suddenly rejected."

The Mormon cricket, *Anabrus simplex* (Orthoptera: [Tettigoniidae]), was another important insect food of the Indians, all over the West. It is not really a cricket, being more closely related to katydids. It is a large insect, about two inches in length, wingless (and it travels in large, dense bands. Bands may be more than a mile wide and several miles long, and with 20-30 or more crickets per square yard. It is sometimes damaging to crops or range vegetation and has been a pest target of the U.S. Department of Agriculture since before the turn of the century. Major Howard Egan[4] described, in his delightful first-person style, a Mormon cricket drive that took place in about . . . The procedure was basically to dig a series of trenches, each [3]0 to 40 feet long and in the shape of a new moon, cover the [trenches] with a thin layer of stiff wheat grass straw, drive the crickets . . . [the] grass covering the trenches, and then set fire to the grass. As . . . begun, Egan thought the Indians were going to a great deal of trouble for a few crickets: "We followed them on horseback and I noticed that there were but very few crickets left behind. As they went down, the line of crickets grew thicker and thicker till the ground ahead of the drivers [men, women and children] was black as coal with the excited, tumbling mass of crickets." After the grass had been fired, Egan observed that in some places the trenches were more than half full of dead crickets: "I went down below the trenches and I venture to say there were not one out of a thousand crickets that passed those trenches . . ."

Once the drive was . . . and children had done their part and were sitting a[round] . . . women gathered the catch into large baskets w[hich they carried] on their backs. We should remember that th[is was in] . . . the days of the women's movement, as Ega[n noted with ad]miration. . . .

SEE A[LSO] . . . [I]NSECT FOOD, P. 2

floating in, but for most of the world's peoples a plate of grubs is considered an inviting and nutritious repast. In Africa, many rural families make their living gathering insects and selling them at farm markets. Mopanie caterpillars (*Gonimbrasia belina*) are so popular that, when in season, they cut into the sale of beef. Movie theaters in Bogota, Colombia, sell roasted big-bottomed ants (*Hormigas culonas*) instead of popcorn. Don Chon's, a popular Mexico City restaurant, is world famous for its insect dishes, based on traditional Aztec recipes. Grasshoppers (Oxya velox) boiled in soy sauce are sold as a luxury item in Japanese supermarkets, and cooked wasps mixed with rice were one of the late Emperor Hirohito's favorite dishes. Edible insects are available in America at shops catering to the Asian community, where you can buy giant water bugs from Thailand and canned silkworm pupae from South Korea.

Gene DeFoliart, Ph.D., professor emeritus of entomology at the University of Wisconsin, has made it something of a personal crusade to break down the western societal taboo against entomophagy, or the eating of insects. He publishes *The Food Insects Newsletter*, an intriguing compilation of historical background, current research, and societal attitudes on the subject. Recipes, too, of course. It comes out three times a year, and has about 2,000 subscribers.

Professor DeFoliart received national attention in 1992, when he was the featured speaker at the New York Entomological Society's 100th Anniversary "Bug Banquet." The $65-a-plate feast offered such delectations as live honeypot ants (so delicious they were strictly one-to-a-customer), wax worm fritters with plum sauce, cricket and vegetable tempura, mealworm balls in zesty tomato sauce, a trail mix of crickets, mealworms and maggots, and California rolls with avocado, rice and fly larvae. For dessert, tollhouse cricket cookies.

Guests attempted to describe the experience. "The tastes are so different and distinctive. A lot of insects taste nutty, like walnuts or sesame seeds. Some taste like shrimp. Some taste meaty, but I can't tell you which meat." Mealworms were compared to "creamy shrimp." The trail mix was "Tasty. Crunchy like potato chips." Fried wax-moth larvae were "a lot like bacon." Crickets were described as "the tofu of the insect world, taking on the taste of whatever they're cooked with." The Thai water bug has "the flavor of lettuce, seaweed, or Gorgonzola cheese, depending on where you bite into it," according to one enthusiast. Another was less enamored of the water bugs, finding them "medicinal." Wax worms were described by a 14-year-old diner as "Kind of juicy—like a fruit candy with juice in the middle. When you bite into them, all the juice comes out." If that doesn't make you want to rush out and try some, nothing will.

DeFoliart hopes that by the year 2000 we will see grocery stores offering a wide variety of edible bugs. There is more than one cookbook on the subject—the best-known is *Entertaining With Insects: The Original Guide to Insect Cookery*, by Ronald Taylor and Barbara Carter. The Insect Club, a restaurant in Washington, D.C., offers a variety of insect dishes to its clientele. Also boding well for the movement is the success of Hot Lix, a transparent tequila-flavored lollipop that comes with a beetle grub inside.

INSTANT FISH KIT

An American icthyologist traveling in Africa made a strange discovery. In a mud puddle, far from any body of water, fish were swimming. How did they get there? The scientist reasoned that the eggs of this particular species must be able to lie dormant in dried-up mud for long periods, then hatch when rainwater soaked their surroundings.

An interesting discovery, no doubt worthy of an article. But how much money can one make writing an article for *Scientific American*? This was an up-to-date scientist, and he knew where the real rewards lay. He contacted the Wham-O Company, who had already made millions from slingshots, Frisbees and Hula Hoops. Why not "Instant

Fish—Just Add Water?" Wham-O leaped to the challenge.

The icthyologist shipped over a large batch of the egg-impregnated mud, and the best scientific minds of Wham-O set about developing a product around them. After eighteen months the Instant Fish Kit was ready and displayed at the 1962 New York Toy Fair. The product was a sensation, guaranteed to provoke melees at the checkout counter as customers swept them from shelves as fast as they could be stocked. Orders poured in to Wham-O's San Gabriel, California, offices.

What happened? As Wham-O executive Richard Knerr put it, "It wasn't until then that we found the fish couldn't produce eggs fast enough to meet the demand. We even tried soft music and air conditioning, but nothing happened, so the whole thing—fish and all—went down the drain."

So Wham-O, birthplace of so many great fads, produced one that remained stuck in the mud.

INTERBANG

In 1967, the American Type Founders Co. introduced the "interbang," an exclamation point (called a "bang" by editors) overstruck with a question mark. It was intended to replace the duel punctuation used at the ends of such emphatic interrogatories as "What the—?!" It has not been seen since.

INVENTIONS, PATENTLY ABSURD

- Simulated Firearm With Pivotally-Mounted Whiskey Glass (U. S. Patent #3,450,403). Point the gun at your mouth and pull the trigger—the 'shot' glass pivots into your mouth. Didn't the Brady Bill finish this kind of thing off?

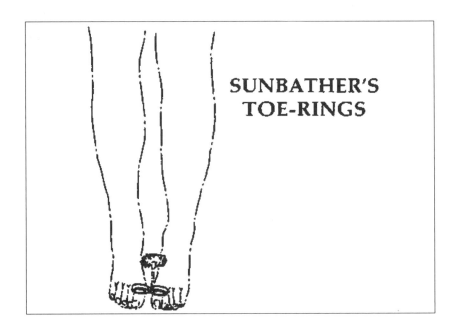

• Baby-Patting Machine (U.S. Patent #3,552,388). Babies are sometimes lulled to sleep by rocking and having their bottoms gently patted. Though automated rockers have been with us for some time, this motorized contraption, which periodically pats the baby's rump, was a first. When the baby moves around and starts having its nose rhythmically patted, the effect is probably no longer comforting.

• Sunbather's Toe Rings were patented in 1973. These were intended to clip the big toes together, preventing the legs from turning outward in repose and thereby insuring the evenness of the tan. The toe-cuffs include a hole in the central connection into which a flower can be placed and meditated upon. Actor and sunbather par excellence George Hamilton might be interested—he was observed in

SUNBATHER'S TOE-RINGS

1992 at the Beverly Hills Hotel placing toothpicks between his toes to get an all-over tan.

- In 1964, a patent was issued for Forget-Me-Not, a device which attaches to the zipper of a small boy's trousers and rings an alarm bell if the fly starts to come open.
- Demonstrated at the Chicago Dental Society meeting in 1966 were dentures which had a photo of the owner laminated into the palate for identification. Presumably helpful if the dentures were lost in a crowd or, worse yet, mixed in with a whole pile of of lost dentures.
- The Sleep Machine. An attempt to capitalize on the fact that many Americans routinely fall asleep in front of the tube, the Sleep Machine featured a TV-like screen on which flickered a soft blue light. Insomniacs were supposed to stare at it until lulled to sleep. But what if it was better than anything else that was on?
- Israel Robert Smuts of Livingston, New Jersey, patented the battery-powered spaghetti fork in 1971. It had a motorized handle which wound the spaghetti around the tines.

J. J. ARMES

In 1973, the Ideal toy company launched the hottest action figure line in its history, based on the motorcycle daredevil Evel Knievel. Figuring that real-life heroes had a proven marketability, three years later it came out with J. J. Armes, world's greatest investigator, also based on an actual person. The real Jay J. Armes was described in the catalog as the world's most successful private eye, who'd never left a case unsolved. He was a multi-millionaire who commanded fees of $50,000 to $250,000 per assignment, and headed a nationwide staff of 2,400 investigators. He owned his own helicopters and airplanes, had a fleet of 11 automobiles, and liked to stroll the grounds of his estate with a cheetah on a leash. He held a black belt in karate, was an expert with a pistol and submachine gun, and had survived 14 attempts on his life. Most remarkable of all, Jay J. Armes had no hands, having lost them in a boyhood accident.

And so Ideal marketed an amputee action figure with two startlingly realistic prosthetic hooks instead of hands. He came with a suitcase full of interchangeable prosthe-

ses, including suction cups, magnets, and a machete.

As inspiring as the real Jaye J. Armes story was, his toy line was D.O.A. For one thing, the work of an actual detective is not that exciting, and unlike Evel Knievel, kids had never heard of him. Secondly, there was the question of taste. It's one thing to admire the real man, another to play with a toy based upon him. As Harold Frankel, a former executive with Ideal explained, "Kids would find it very difficult to role-play a man with two artificial arms. I don't even think you'd want to. I would be squeamish about it myself."

By the way, Ideal's Evel Knievel line crashed and burned shortly afterward, following the impetuous daredevil's baseball bat attack on his former press agent.

JOEY STIVIC DOLL

J. J. Armes wasn't Ideal's only flop in 1976.

In the mid-1970s *All in the Family* was America's favorite show, and when Archie Bunker's daughter Gloria had a baby, a toy tie-in seemed like a sure-fire winner. As the Ideal catalog put it: "Remember when *I Love Lucy* had a baby on TV? Remember the excitement it created? Why,

it was almost as though the whole country was having the baby. There hasn't been anything like it since. Not until now. Because now Mike and Gloria have had a baby, ARCHIE BUNKER'S GRANDSON, Joey Stivic..." The catalog went on to underscore the enormous play the baby would get on the top-rated show, thereby promoting the product.

Only one thing kept the adorable, 14" drink-and-wet Joey Stivic doll from

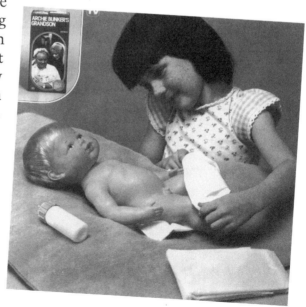

selling—his penis. Within a few years, anatomically-correct male dolls sold well, but Joey was too far ahead of the curve. Then again, the type of people who would buy Archie Bunker's Grandson just may not have been the type who want their daughter's dolls to have penises, then or ever.

KUDZU

Kudzu was introduced into the United States by the Japanese at the 1876 Philadelphia Exposition. They prized it for its edible roots and made cloth and paper from its fibrous stems and leaves. With its thick foliage and purple wysteria-like flowers, it became popular in the south as the "porch vine."

Kudzu is not easy to cultivate. It has to be grown from carefully-nurtured seedlings, and even those are delicate and compete poorly with other weeds. Nevertheless, in the 1930s and 1940s, kudzu was promoted widely for the many benefits it offered. As a hearty, fast-growing ground cover it would help prevent soil erosion, and its deep, extensive root system would replenish nitrogen in farmed-out soil. Nutritionally comparable to alfalfa, it even provided forage for cattle. Great efforts were made to establish it in the warm, sunny climes it requires. The Soil Conservation Service distributed it free to farmers. Railroads and highway departments peppered their right-of-ways with millions of the seedlings. Communities engaged in planting projects and kudzu clubs were cheerleading for "the savior of the South."

Any fan of cataclysmic science-fiction could have seen it coming. Foolish humans—once again they have tampered with alien forces beyond their comprehension! Kudzu can grow a foot a day, dividing at nodes spaced every foot or so along its stem. Within a season, a single kudzu stem can grow a hundred feet in every direction and cover the ground eight feet deep, casting a living net over everything in its path. And every spring it starts all over again. Some claimed kudzu grew faster than a man could run, only a slight exaggeration. It reminds one of the relentless hunger displayed by swarming killer ants or the blob in the movies—except this is occurring in *real* life. Trees, gardens, utility poles, buildings, and cars parked too long are transformed into topiary. It has been suggested that Amelia Earhart may have tried to taxi her plane through a pasture on which kudzu had designs, and that Jimmy Hoffa may have taken a too-leisurely stroll through a leafy glade.

As the plant's imperialistic designs were exposed, "kudzu clubs" became a shameful memory. The energy that had gone into promoting the rampaging weed was now directed to stopping its spread. Axes, chainsaws, fire and chemical poisons have all been employed in the battle, to little avail. Kudzu covers millions of acres in 12 states of the American South, mostly concentrated around the old farms, highways and railroads where it was once so enthusiastically sown. It kills the trees it covers by blocking off their sunlight, and shorts out the lines on utility poles. It costs the region about $50 million annually in lost farm and timber production. The former "miracle vine" has earned such nicknames as foot-a-night, Jack-and-the-beanstalk and mile-a-minute. Poet James Dickey termed it "a vegetal form of cancer."

As Southerners have noted, "Cows won't eat kudzu, but kudzu will eat a cow."

THE LIVING GARAGE

"What is a Living Garage? It is an enclosed area which provides you with new space for entertaining, for play, for hobbies and for displaying the family's pride and joy—the car."

In April, 1958, *House & Garden* promoted the "living garage" as one of the most important new trends in suburban living. As the article put it, "Today's automobiles are are not only designed to be looked at but...they are easy to live with." Considering that these dream

131

machines might be traded in every year or two for the latest style, wasn't it a shame to let them languish in the garage? Why not make them the centerpiece of a room?

The Living Garage (the term is always capitalized in the article) was to use materials and colors that one would expect to find in the rest of the house. Over the entry, a "vinyl-coated nylon awning;" inside, "soft brown quarry tile flooring... walls of glass and Citron yellow Panelyte..." Around the car the homeowner could arrange potted plants and casual furniture. The room would be used for children's parties, TV, and informal entertaining.

Four design concepts were presented, one making the garage into a children's wing of the house, with a swing, climbing bars, and a maze painted on the floor for tag games. Clear the deck when daddy pulls in!

Why didn't this trend catch on? Just think of the way your garage floor looks by the middle of winter when all those sand-laden ice chunks have fallen off the car and melted. Then there's oil leaks, gasoline fumes, and carbon monoxide poisoning. And where do you put that can of gas and all those oily rags? There's got to be some room in the home set aside for chaos.

LOST CAUSES

The seventeen-pound *Encyclopedia of Associations* lists thousands of organizations dedicated to many different causes, including some in which defeat might have been gracefully conceded some time ago. The following list is drawn from *Organized Obsessions*, by Deborah Burek and Martin Connors.

Americans for Decency— A group of individuals and organizations dedicated to the motto "Decency Belongs Everywhere" is behind the Americans for Decency Postage Stamp Project, which is petitioning the U.S. Postal Service to issue an Americans for Decency Stamp. Urges boycotts of theaters that "have no sense of decency in their shows." Objects to the "loud and vulgar so-called music with suggestive lyrics that is constantly broadcast." This cause was lost when Elvis clobbered Pat Boone.

Best Candidate Committee— Attempts to improve the quality of Congress by encouraging the selection of the "best" candidates for office. Isn't that what we have PACs for?

Campaign for World Government— Works for the establishment of a universal world federation, democratically-structured with a civilian police force. It's open to all nations which are willing to accept and abide by an overall constitution. Could perhaps be headquartered in the former Yugoslavia?

Citizens for a Debt-Free America— Encourages American citizens and groups to make private contributions to the U.S. Treasury to help roll back our nearly five-trillion dollar national debt. Encourages legislators to work toward retiring the debt by the year 2000. Contributions toward that end have amounted to over $12 million in the last ten years. Don't work out the math—it's too depressing.

Cowsills Fan Club— Celebrates the career of the 1970s family singing group, famous for their squeaky-clean rendition of the theme from *Hair*, and their hit *The Rain, The Park, and Other Things*. The club publishes a newsletter which keeps fans apprised of the Cowsills' public appearances.

Ernest Fan Club— Celebrates the noted comedian and film star who set the standard by which all forms of brainless entertainment are measured. Publishes *KnoWhutImean? News*.

International Stop Continental Drift Society— A real group, but just pulling our leg.

Martin van Buren Fan Club— Fans of the eighth President of the U. S. seek to bring attention to "the many outstanding and positive things which he did during his lifetime." You'll have to subscribe to their newsletter, *OK News*, if you want to find out what those things might be.

Monarchist Alliance— Believes that a Christian monarchy is not only the divinely intended form of government but one which would be far preferable to what we have now. Works to reestablish a constitutional monarchy in the U. S. A possible front group for the Ross Perot campaign?

National Society for the Prevention of Cruelty to Mushrooms— An organization seeking to improve the lot of various neglected or mistreated life forms. A serious organization? Who can say anymore.

Pia Zadora Fan Club— A fan club for the pixieish,

baby-faced actress and singer who has appeared on the Tonight Show and television commercials, as well as in several films in which she takes all her clothes off.

Society for the Eradication of Television (SET)— Encourages members to "Just Say No to Television," the viewing addiction that consumes 3.5 billion hours a day of human consciousness globally. Publishes *S.E.T. Free, The Newsletter Against Television.* Says spokesperson Pat Brown, "The only thing to do with a television set is turn it off and throw it out the window." S.E.T. members do not own televisions, and consider watching TV to be an electronic form of lobotomy. S.E.T. believes that television retards the inner life of human beings, destroys human interaction, squanders time and draws viewers into abject addiction. Furthermore, it distorts real life, promotes mindless consumption and greed, instills bourgeois complacency and fosters racism, heterosexism, lookism and ageism. True enough, but without television how would we know about Pia Zadora?

Stop War Toys Campaign— A project of the War Resisters League that protests the glamorization of violence through toys. Haven't they seen that bumper sticker popular with five-year-old boys— "I Will Give Up My Toy Gun When You Pry It From My Hot, Sticky, Little Fingers"?

Tax Free America— The name alone chills a Democrat's heart. The group wishes to end all federal, state, county and municipal taxes and replace them with a two percent national sales tax.

United States Korfball Association— Seeks to promote interest in the popular Dutch sport. Described as "similar to basketball," Korfball calls for two teams, of two men and two women each, to be placed on opposite sides of the court, one playing offense and the other defense. The rules forbid blocking, dribbling, or running with the ball, but for information as to exactly what you *can* do with the ball, you will have to contact the association.

Witches Anti-Discrimination Lobby— Promotes a better image for witches. Agitates to make Halloween a legal paid holiday for practitioners of witchcraft. Something about a political lobby for witches is annoying. After all, if they don't like things the way they are, why don't they just *change* them.

MALABATE PR105

By 1965, pollution caused by automobile exhaust was a growing national concern. It had even been given a catchy name: smog. Albert Verley and Co. of New Jersey announced a new product intended to alleviate the problem. The impressively-named Malabate PR105 was a fuel additive that promised to make diesel fumes smell like talcum powder. But the smell of talcum powder is not intended to mask the smell of a dirty diaper, so perhaps it's best that it never caught on.

MARK TWAIN, INVENTOR

Mark Twain was fascinated by the great inventors who were remaking the world during his lifetime. "An inventor," he wrote, "is a poet—a true poet—and nothing in any degree less than a high order of poet." Twain's own endeavors in the poetry of invention were doggerel at best. He achieved mild success with a self-adhesive scrapbook in which the pages were covered with a glue which, when wetted, held the clippings in place. He also came up with an elastic strap with buttonholes at each end, which was supposed to help adjust vests, corsets and trousers to size.

In the 1880s, Twain came up with what he regarded as his best idea, "Mark Twain's Memory Builder." Players were issued a board with historical periods indicated on it. When monarchs, wars or minor events were called out, the player had to stick pins on the timeline at the appropriate period. Different versions of the game could focus on particular subjects and periods, such as the French Revolution, Canada,

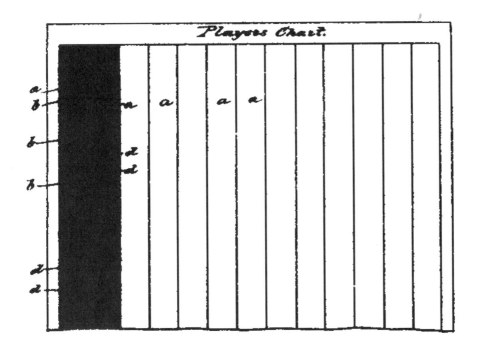

world authors, and of course, names and nationalities of inventors. Twain wrote enthusiastically about his idea to a friend, Joe Twichell. Perhaps considering it one of Twain's gentle satires, Twichell passed the letter along to the Hartford *Courant*, which printed it. Twain was enraged at this breach of confidence—the idea could have been stolen by anyone seeing it in the paper! The fact that no one bothered to do so should have been a tip off, but Twain was convinced of the Memory Builder's appeal. He got it patented (U.S. Patent # 324,535, 1885), and a few years later had it put out by his own publishing company. Needless to say...

Twain lost a good deal of money investing in other people's bad ideas, including Kaolatype, an engraving process, and Plasmon, a milk-based health food. Perhaps the strangest was the "bed clamp," designed to keep infants from kicking off their blankets or rolling out of bed. As Twain saw it, its only drawback was that it was too cheap, but felt that he could correct that shortcoming easily enough. His publisher was pressed into service testing it on his own child, but found that the clamp tended to tear up the bed sheets. After devoting an inordinate amount of time to the project, Twain finally threw in the towel.

Having lost $42,000 on one patent, he wrote, "I gave it away to a man whom I had long detested and whose family I desired to ruin."

THE MILE HIGH BUILDING

Architectural genius Frank Lloyd Wright is famous for his Fallingwater house and the Guggenheim Museum. His most most audacious design, though, was never executed.

In 1956, Wright unveiled at a press conference a 26-foot long rendering of a building he called Mile-High Illinois. If constructed, the 528-story building would have been nearly four times as tall as the 1,454 foot Sears Tower in Chicago, currently the world's tallest. Atomic-powered tandem elevator cabs would run up the outside of the building on ratchet-guided tracks. There would be two decks accommodating 150 helicopters and covered parking for 15,000 cars. Wright estimated that the building would cost $100 million, half of which would be required to house the building's 130,000 workers at conventional sites. He envisioned that ten such buildings would supply all the office space required by New York City. Existing structures could be torn down and replaced by parks and recreation facilities. "No one can afford to build it now," he said, "but in the future no one can afford *not* to build it." He also said that, "The Mile High would absorb, justify and legitimize the gregarious instinct of humanity."

Unconvincingly, Wright claimed that the lightweight, rapier-like design would have no sway, even at its peak. There are ordinary 40-story buildings that sway alarmingly in high winds; how a mile-high building would avoid this problem in The Windy City is unclear. Maintenance personnel and firefighters foresaw insoluble problems in the idea. Whether people would actually find it appealing to work in such a structure was not even discussed.

Within a year, Wright was offering an almost equally offbeat idea to the citizens of Arizona for their state capitol. This time he was promoting a single level building that would spread offices over a vast horizontal level. "Vertical is vertigo, in human life," Wright wrote, "The horizontal line is the life-line of humanity."

But then, we all know what another genius said about foolish consistencies and small minds.

"THE MOST WONDERFUL STORY" DOLL

In 1957 Ben Michtom, the president of the Ideal Toy Company, visited the Vatican while on a European tour. He met the Pope and was so inspired by the experience that he decided Ideal should market a Baby Jesus doll. Though he himself was Jewish, it seemed to him obvious that Christian children would love to have a doll based on the central figure in their religion. He received a favorable response from religious leaders he talked to about the idea and even secured the pontiff's blessing. Reaction back home at the toy factory was considerably less enthusiastic, but Ben Michtom was a man possessed. Brushing aside all objections, he brought out the doll under the name of "The Most Wonderful Story." It came packaged in what looked like a large, ornately-bound Bible. Inside, the Jesus doll lay on a bed of straw surrounded by cardboard figures of the Holy Family.

Ideal was an industry giant known for its success with dolls. It put its considerable weight behind The Most Wonderful Story, so even skeptical buyers ended up ordering large quantities. Their skepticism was soon justified. Baby Jesus dolls collected dust on toy store shelves all over the country. One store devoted a full-page newspaper ad to it and as a result sold all of six.

What happened? Christian parents were reluctant to buy their children a baby Jesus, knowing the rough and disrespectful treatment to which children's playthings are routinely subjected. The idea of the Christ child being dressed and undressed, dragged down the stairs by one foot, thrown in a bin with other toys or left out in the yard in the rain did not appeal to them. Merchants were also perplexed as to how they should handle the unsalable item. "How can you mark down Jesus Christ?" they asked.

Accepting their responsibility for one of the great mistakes in toy history, Ideal agreed to buy the dolls back from dealers. What ultimately happened to them is subject of speculation in the toy business. One unsubstantiated rumor has it that they were broken up and the body parts sold to pilgrims as holy relics.

NAME FLOPS: FOREIGN

Some foreign companies blithely enter the American market with names that are a bit jarring, like the German industrial giants, Siemens and FAG. Here are some others that will probably not be so lucky until they consider new names:

• A Finnish brewer briefly exported two new labels to the United States: "Siff" beer and "Koff" beer.

• A gourmet chocolate and fruit confection is sold in the United States under its German name, "Zit!"

• The name of a popular fermented milk drink sold in Japan is pronounced "Kowpis."

• A Chinese patent medicine, identified as a "blood nourishing paste," is sold under the name "Ass Glue."

• "Fockink" is the name of a Dutch liqueur.

• "Homo Sausage" is the brand name of a beef jerky sold in Japan.

- "Mucos" is a Japanese soft drink.
- "Pipi" is the unfortunate name of an orangeade sold in Yugoslavia.
- "Pshitt" is a French carbonated beverage.
- "Trim Pecker" is the name of a line of trousers sold in Japan.
- Chocolate-covered ice cream bars are sold in Germany under the brand name "Prick."
- A Chinese candy goes by the name "Strange Taste."
- A writing tablet sold for little girls in Taiwan, illustrated with a cloying rendition of a sweet little moppet, is called "Little Hussy."

- The most popular toothpaste in much of the Far East, until recently, was marketed under the name "Darkie Toothpaste." The package said (in Chinese) "Black man Tooth Paste" and the logo featured what appeared to be a smiling Al Jolson in blackface wearing a top hat.
- Sumitomo, a Japanese steel firm, took out full-page ads in American trade magazines to promote its special-purpose steel pipe, called Sumitomo High Toughness. They used a Japanese agency to develop the ads, which abbreviated the name and ran the

abbreviation in bold type over three-quarters of the page: SHT. Beneath this eye-catching banner was the message that the product "was made to match its name."

NAME FLOPS: AMERICAN

Lest we think we do any better, some of the most commonplace American brand names and advertising slogans do not travel well either.

- When McDonald's began opening outlets in France, it translated its "Big Mac" hamburger as *Gros Mec.* In French slang, that means "big pimp." Hunt-Wesson had a similar problem introducing its Big John line into Canada. It translated as *Gros Jos,* a slang expression for large breasts.
- A beer company's slogan, "Turn it loose," translated into Spanish as "Our beer causes diarrhea."
- Fresca was marketed under its American name in Mexico until it learned that "fresca" was a slang term for lesbian.
- Perdue Chicken uses the slogan, "It takes a tough man to make a tender chicken." In Spanish this translated as "It takes a sexually-excited man to make a chicken sensual."
- The Chevy Nova was not a big hit with the Spanish-speaking. Translated literally, its name means "Star." When spoken, though it sounds like "no va," or "it doesn't go."
- Similar problems were had by the Ford "Fiera" (in Spanish, "ugly old woman"), and the Ford "Pinto" (Brazilian slang for "small penis").
- Still in Spanish, a cigarette which wanted to advertise that it had less tar turned out to be claiming to have "less asphalt."
- When Pet milk was marketed in France, its makers were soon informed that "pet" in French means "to break wind."

- The Johnson Company's Pledge was sold in Holland under its American name. Unfortunately, in Dutch, the name means "piss."
- "Come Alive", Pepsi's slogan during the 1960s, came out in German as "Arise From the Dead!" In a similar vein, "Coke Adds Life" translated into Chinese became "Coke Brings Your Ancestors Back From the Dead."
- In the 1920s, when Coca-Cola was planning its marketing strategy in China, it hoped to use its corporate name. It discovered that Coca-Cola pronounced phonetically in Chinese means either "Female Horse Stuffed with Wax," or, with a slightly different intonation, "Bite the Wax Tadpole."
- Kentucky Fried Chicken's slogan, "It's finger-lickin' good!" translated to Chinese as "You'll eat your fingers!"

NATIONAL BOWLING LEAGUE

"The National Bowling League, one of the most expensive experiments in the history of professional sports, got off to a fair start at the Bronco Bowl tonight. In the premiere performance of this nationwide ten-team league, the Dallas Broncos met the New York Gladiators before about 2,000 persons."
The New York Times, October 13, 1961

The National Bowling League was predicated on the hope that throngs of Americans would pay admission to watch professional bowling leagues compete. The New York Gladiators, Dallas Broncos, Kansas City Stars, Detroit Thunderbirds and six other teams each played out of a specially-designed, multi-million dollar arena. The Bronco Bowl, three miles out of Dallas, had seats eighteen rows deep in a semi-circle behind six bowling lanes. There was even a seven-piece jazz band on the side, which according to

The New York Times, "kept things noisy between matches." The arena could seat 2,500 at prices from $1 to $3, though on opening night the Bronco Bowl owner was disappointed to note that his arena was not filled up. Needless to say, it didn't get any better. The NBL folded within the year.

The National Bowling League joined such other failed sports franchises as the Federal League (the upstart baseball league that brought about the court ruling in 1922 that exempted baseball from antitrust statutes), the American Basketball League, and most recently, the USFL (United States Football League).

NEW COKE

"Coca-Cola is the sublimated essence of all that America stands for. A decent thing, honestly made, universally distributed and conscientiously improved with the years." This quote, from an homage which appeared in the *Gazette* of Emporia, Kansas, was a favorite of Robert Woodruff, who ran the Coca-Cola Company from the 1920s until the 1970s. The extent to which Coca-Cola had been "conscientiously improved" since 1903, when the company succeeded in removing the last minute amounts of cocaine, was minimal. True, corn syrup had replaced cane sugar, but that had not altered the flavor. Why mess with success? For decades Coca-Cola ruled the soft drink market. From the twenties, Woodruff saw to it that Coke was "within arm's reach of desire" anywhere and everywhere in America—not only at soda fountains and restaurants, but at gas stations, factories, offices, movie theaters and baseball parks. The Coca-Cola logo became a ubiquitous American icon, and strict quality control ensured that its distinctive taste was consistent nationwide. When Coke opened foreign markets, suggestions that it adapt to differing national tastes were rebuffed by Woodruff, who had confidence in the universal appeal of Coke's secret formula. In a marketing masterstroke, Woodruff saw to it that Coke followed

American servicemen overseas. "See that every man in uniform gets a bottle of Coca-Cola for five cents wherever he is and whatever it costs the company," he ordered in 1941. In the course of the war, GIs drank five billion bottles, and the taste was a tangible link with home.

In 1898, thirteen years after pharmacist John Styth Pemberton concocted Coke's formula, another pharmacist, Caleb Bradham, developed the mixture of kola-nut extract and "rare oils" that would come to be called Pepsi-Cola. In 1972 Pepsi went *mano a mano*, pitting its flavor against Coke's in the "Pepsi Challenge," a blind taste-test that claimed most people preferred Pepsi. In an attempt to disprove Pepsi's results, Coca-Cola conducted its own private taste tests—and discovered to its horror that Pepsi was telling the truth! Within a few years Pepsi was outselling Coke at supermarkets, which accounted for a third of soft drink sales. Coke's lucrative contracts with fast

COCA-COLA EXECUTIVES ROBERTO GOIZUETA AND DONALD KEOUGH UNVEIL NEW COKE AT A PRESS CONFERENCE IN 1985.

food outlets hinged on its number one position—if it lost that status, it would lose those contracts. Coca-Cola executives obsessed over the threat Pepsi posed. Coke was more widely distributed and outspent Pepsi on advertising by $150 million; still Pepsi's market share grew. Obviously the problem was the product. If Coke's taste was truly not number one, how long could Coke itself remain so?

By the end of the 1970s, Coca-Cola executives began thinking the unthinkable: to revise the sacred text known as Merchandise 7X, the formula locked in the vault of the Trust Company of Georgia that was so secret it was known to no more than three people at any time. In September, 1983, Coca-Cola launched Project Kansas (portentiously named for the quote from the Emporia, Kansas *Gazette* editorial) to study the possibility of changing Coke's taste. It was necessary to test reaction not only to a reformulated Coke, but even to the *idea* of a reformulated Coke. The former was a far easier sell than the latter. "It was like saying you were going to make the flag prettier," admitted one executive. The immutable taste of Coca-Cola was a fixed star in the constellation of American culture, even among those who did not always choose Coke over Pepsi. Nevertheless, when a new, sweeter formula was developed that consistently out-tested both Pepsi and the old Coke, what was the company to do with it? It could be marketed as a second Coke, but that evaded the issue. Coke had to be the best-tasting Cola in the world, and if this new formula tasted better, it should be the flagship brand. What's more, two different Cokes would just compete with each other and put Pepsi in the number one spot—an intolerable outcome. Late in 1984, the decision was made. The 95-year-old Woodruff, close to death, acquiesced. The formula Merchandise 7X would be retired; Merchandise 7X-100 would replace it. New Coke was born.

Total secrecy surrounded the decision. A special suite of offices was rented for the advertising crew, with a guard at the door to see to it that no unauthorized persons entered and a shredder to ensure that no scrap left. Gradually, key executives were let in on the plan on a "need-to-know" basis, while disinformation was used to keep industry watchers off the scent. Firms that developed the promotional materials and packaging were told that if they let the secret out they would never work for Coca-Cola again, a death sentence for an Atlanta-area business. Coke executives met with outside suppliers in parking lots in the middle of the night, where art and copy were examined by flashlight.

With four days advance notice, Coca-Cola scheduled a press conference for April 23, 1985 to announce "the most significant soft-drink marketing development in the company's nearly 100-year history." The press conference, held at Lincoln Center in New York City, was carefully orchestrated. The event began with a multi-screen testimonial to the greatness of Coke, linking it to every aspect of the American experience from JFK to the Grand Canyon, and from cowboys and kids to the Statue of Liberty. This kind of approach doesn't tend to wow the press, and after Chairman of the Board Roberto Goizueta and President Donald Keough finished their presentation, telling reporters that "the best has been made even better," they had some tough questions. Despite all the preparation, Goizueta and Keough did not have good answers.

What was the new taste like? Goizueta: "I would say that it is smoother, uh, uh, rounder, yet, uh, yet, bolder... it has a more *harmonious* flavor."

Wasn't it just a response to the Pepsi Challenge? Goizueta: "Oh, gosh, no. That's, uh... the Pepsi Challenge? When did that happen?"

What about the thirty-nine percent of people who prefer the old Coke? Keough: "Well, thirty-nine percent of the people voted for McGovern..."

And, of course, the question to which there was no good answer: if it ain't broke, why fix it? New Coke's sweeter formula was tacit admission that Pepsi had the better taste, and Coke had to reformulate its product to become more like Pepsi. No alternate scenarios could obfuscate the obvious, and Pepsi immediately began rubbing Coke's corporate nose in it. Pepsi declared a corporate holiday, V-C Day, for Victory over Coke. It took out full-page newspaper ads declaring in part: "After 87 years of going at it eyeball to eyeball the other guy just blinked. Coca-Cola is withdrawing their product from the marketplace, and reformulating Coke to be more like Pepsi... Maybe they finally realized what most of us have known for years. Pepsi tastes better than Coke."

Coca-Cola executives knew that the soft-drink's loyal fans would object to the change, but felt they'd fall in line soon enough. They were hardly prepared for the outrage of a public that felt betrayed. Their 800 lines were flooded with complaints. Customers complained that new Coke was too sweet, tasted flat, diluted, and lacked Coke's characteristic "bite." Comparisons ranged from "furniture polish," to "sewer water," to worst of all, "two-day-old Pepsi." *San Francisco Examiner* columnist Bill Mandel called it "Coke for wimps" and lamented the loss of that "battery acid" tang. (Close enough: that tang actually comes from carefully controlled levels of phosphoric acid.) Jim Fitzgerald of the *Detroit Free Press* mocked Coke's claim that the new drink was "smoother, rounder, bolder" by asking what the old Coke was—"lumpy, square and bashful?"

Old Coke connoisseurs began hoarding cases of their cherished brew, some taking time off from work, cashing in savings and prowling the boondocks in search of The Real Thing. A Beverly Hills wine shop laid in 500 cases in the classic 6 1/2 oz glass bottles. At $30 a case (three times the list price) they quickly sold out, even Federal Expressing an order to a Montreal customer. One Hollywood producer with a discerning palate rented a wine locker to store his 100 cases of vintage stock.

Gay Mullins, a Seattle medical researcher, founded the Old Coke Drinkers of America to pressure Coca-Cola into bringing back the original formula. He invested $45,000 of his own money to print up T shirts (new Coke with the circle-slash symbol over it), fund a direct-mail campaign, and set up a phone bank to take the calls of like-minded Cokaholics. He staged protest rallies and planned a class action suit. When asked why he devoted his energies to this of all causes he replied: "Somebody had to do it. You have to be ever vigilant in our democracy. When they took Old Coke off the market they violated my freedom of choice. It's as basic as the Magna Charta, the Declaration of Independence. We went to war with Japan over that freedom."

The marketing manager for Coca-Cola bottling in Roanoke, Virginia, received a letter from a woman expressing an even higher level of devotion. It read in part: "There are only two things in my life: God and Coca-Cola. Now you have taken one of those things away from me."

Against this barrage, the Coca-Cola Company stonewalled. When asked if there was a chance they would bring back the old formula, they replied, "Never." And despite the bad publicity, their decision still made sense. In taste tests, consumers consistently preferred new Coke over both old Coke and Pepsi. (Despite his professed fervor, even Gay Mullins was unable to distinguish the taste of new Coke from old, or even from R C Cola.) The company had been prepared for negative stories, but expected them to die down in a week or two. It was only a soft-drink, for gosh sake...

But the negative stories continued week after week, in newspapers, magazines and on television news programs. While they defended themselves on the basis of taste, Coca-Cola executives began to realize that the opposition was rooted in resistance to the change itself. Todd Gitlin, a University of California, Berkeley, professor, suggested that Americans often identify with products to compensate for our culture's rootlessness. In a world of ceaseless change, people require some constants. For some people the constant was Coke. It was their rock of ages, something that had remained unchanged from their childhoods. One letter to Coca-Cola mournfully described, "The sorrow I feel knowing not only won't I ever enjoy the Real Coke, but my children and grandchildren won't either...I guess my children will have to take my word for it." In the eyes of these consumers, the Coca-Cola Company had violated a sacred trust. Some of the callers to Coca-Cola's hotline "Sounded as if we'd killed God," said one executive, adding, "You can't reassure people about killing God." Coca-Cola executives began to worry. Had they poisoned a well of good feeling that had existed for their company? Coca-Cola was being described as arrogant. Executives could not even attend social gatherings without being assailed by new Coke critics. By mid-June, sales were down. Morale at the company was plummeting as executives, salespeople, even those manning the hotline lost confidence in new Coke.

The stonewall crumbled. On July 10, 1985, Coca-Cola announced that it would return its original formula soft-drink to the market under the name Classic Coke. ABC interrupted *General Hospital* to break the news, and devoted its *Nightline* program to the topic. Senator Pryor of Arkansas expressed his jubilation on the Senate floor. Coca-Cola's hotline received eighteen thousand grateful calls that day. One woman told the operator that she had just found out that she was pregnant, and didn't know what would make her husband happier—the news that he would be a father or the news that old Coke was back.

New Coke was dubbed "The Edsel of the Eighties," a new paradigm of the supreme flop. In some markets it was outsold by Coke Classic as much as nine to one. In 1986, McDonalds switched its fountains from the new version to Classic, as did Hardees. In 1989, the new Coke was renamed Coke II and is still sold in some markets, at the discretion of the local bottler. At the end of 1993, Coke Classic was the best-selling brand of soft-drink, leading Pepsi by a market share of 20.1 to 17.7. Seeing that the net result of the whole episode was to propell Coca-Cola to the forefront of the national consciousness, there are some who believe that the whole episode was a Machiavellian plot. To those suspicions, Coca-Cola President Don Keough responded, "We're not that smart and we're not that stupid."

NEW VIETNAM

What more inviting place to take the family while vacationing in Florida than a theme park recreating the Vietnam War? So thought the Rev. Carl McIntire, a fundamentalist New Jersey preacher, when he set out to build New Vietnam.

"The Vietnamese village will be over to the left, and the Special Forces 'A' attachment camp will be to the right," he told a *Newsweek* reporter visiting his site in September, 1975.

"The village will be authentic. Rice paddies, ducks, chickens, those animals with humps on their backs—

151

what do you call them? The whole bit," added his assistant, Giles Pace, a former Green Beret. Best of all, it would be populated with genuine Vietnamese. As the war ended in 1974, Vietnamese refugees began settling in Florida, mostly middle-class businessmen, artisans, and former Air Force officers and their families. MacIntire, a pro-Vietnam war activist, had organized victory marches on Washington, sponsoring 56 of them. He set up a craft outlet, Viet Arts, for which the Vietnamese produced ceramic elephants, flags, Christmas trees and hand-woven rugs. But MacIntire saw a brighter future. His Reformation Freedom Center owned 300 acres complete with five abandoned buildings in the area of Cape Canaveral, and it occurred to him to transform it into a Vietnamese theme park staffed by the refugees.

Blueprints were drawn up and work commenced. Banana and palm trees were planted for atmosphere. There were to be paddies with irrigation dykes, water buffalo (the ones with the humps on their backs) and other assorted farm animals, all enclosed in a moat which could be used to ferry tourists on sampan rides (heads down—it's that *Apocalypse Now* river boat!). The village was to contain sixteen fake thatched huts, and the buildings, which would be made over to resemble upper-class Vietnamese homes, would double as Viet Arts outlets and restaurants serving authentic cuisine.

Next door would be the Special Forces compound, complete with trenches, mortar emplacements, bunkers, and a concrete blockhouse housing a weapons museum. In addition to the four-foot-high sandbag wall bristling with fake machine guns, the compound was to be surrounded by crisscrossed barbed wire, punji stakes, and fake Claymore mines.

The camp was supposed to open in the winter of 1975, just in time for the tourist season. At regular intervals a speaker system would fill the air with the crackle of automatic fire, the thump of mortars, and the screams of civilians. Park staff dressed as GIs would fire blanks at an unseen enemy. Tourists who got into the spirit could plant themselves behind a dummy machine gun or dive into bunkers for cover.

"Tourists are going to love this," insisted McIntire, "and every penny is going to go back to the Vietnamese. The Bible says love your neighbor. We're taking them in our arms and giving them our love."

Pace was more pragmatic. "They'll work anywhere for a paycheck," he said of the refugees.

Those paychecks never materialized, as New Vietnam was never completed. Only with the release of *Rambo* could we experience the Vietnam War as a fantasyland.

NO FRILLS BOOKS

The late 1970s saw the appearance of a mysterious new line of products in the nation's supermarkets. "No frills" or "generic" merchandise came in stark white packages, with unadorned black lettering describing the contents: "Peas," "Bleach," "Tea Bags." Beneath the identification was a description of the contents that avoided sell-words such as "taste-tempting" or "succulent" in favor of such blunt admissions as "beans may not be uniform in color or texture." Even beer, cigarettes, and Scotch whiskey were sold under the no-name label. The category captured 5% of the market by 1981, with many retailing experts expecting generics to account for 25% of sales within a few years.

Possibly the strangest manifestation of the no-frills trend was Jove Pubishing's 1981 line of no-frills books. The four titles offered were *Western*, *Science Fiction*, *Romance* and *Mystery*. Their covers were white with their generic titles printed in the characteristic black, boxy type. No author's name was given, of course; each book was a compendium of all the most dependable clichés of its genre. Product contents were listed in the deadpan style; readers were assured that *Romance* contained "a kiss, a promise, a misunderstanding, another kiss, a happy ending."

The New York Times reviewed the series under the

title "Review, complete with everything: pompous theories, big words, obscure literary references, reviewer's personal axe to grind." The *Times* did protest that the little tomes were, unlike their supermarket equivalents, no bargain. Each 60-page booklet sold for $1.50, about half the cost of a James Michener effort ten times as long, and not much less generic.

OOBIE

High on the list of truly inexplicable toys was Parker Brothers' Oobie. Oobie was brought out in the early 1970s, in a confused attempt to tap into the counter-culture zeitgeist. Oobie was a clam-like plastic container with cartoon eyes painted on the top of it. It opened to hold a written message, and there was a place to write an address on the outside. The child was supposed to write a message to a friend, place it in Oobie, and put the friend's address on the outside. The child was then to leave Oobie—anywhere. Anyone who came by and happened to be headed in the direction indicated on the address, be it across town or across the country, was supposed to pick up Oobie and help him on his journey, hitch-hiker style. After a series of adventures, Oobie would arrive at his destination and the message would be delivered. Far out!

Most parents, even in that more innocent age, did not like the idea that some pervert finding the Oobie would not only get their child's address, but be equipped with a splendid excuse to drop by. Parker Brothers quickly got the message—Oobie was a dead letter.

PAPER DRESSES

You could scoop a neckline or raise its hemline with a quick snip of the scissors, and repair it with Scotch Tape. No more dry-cleaning bills—all it needs is a few swipes of an eraser. Good for three to ten wearings, "depending on

the clemency of the weather and the intensity of the wearer's frug," in *Time* magazine's 1966-vintage words. And when you tired of it, crumple it up and throw it out. It was the paper dress, one of the most ephemeral expressions of sixties consciousness.

Paper dresses were developed by the Scott Paper Company, and offered by mail for $1.25 to promote its "Color Explosion" line of towels, napkins and toilet tissue. As the press release put it:

"Now every girl can have a paper dress to call her own. For the first time ever, paper is being made into dresses for real dolls—teenage girls. These "Paper Capers" are brightly printed skimps for beach and play. Made from specially-prepared paper with a crisp, waffly textured surface, they are treated for fire resistance and sell for $1.25 each. A girl might wear a Caper to her next patio party, then for a few outings at the beach, and then get to work with her scissors! She can cut it down to a tunic, then a shell, then to unusual place mats."

The styling of the sleeveless shifts was strictly paper bag and they were available in only two prints, paisley and op art. But when Scott received 500,000 orders in six months, the fashion industry flew into a tizzy. After filling its orders Scott discontinued production, not wanting to be involved in dress manufacturing, but others quickly stepped in to meet the demand.

These other designs were far more ambitious. The Mars Manufacturing Corporation of Asheville, North Carolina, quickly became the top producer, selling 80,000 per week. Sterling Paper Products expected to gross $6 million in 1967 with $8 maternity dresses and $15 wedding gowns in its line, the latter being an appropriate application of the one-use-only concept. In the works was a $12 man's suit. Sterling had another clever notion: paper resort wear. Vacationers could fly off with minimal luggage, pick up a paper wardrobe when they arrived, then throw it away before returning home. For those of sublime confidence, there were specially-treated paper bikinis.

The Hallmark greeting card company offered a complete party kit: a floral-print shirt with matching cups, plates, place mats, napkins, matches and (as would be expected) invitations.

Foil dresses were popular, as well as a paint-it-yourself white dress that came with a set of paints. In her Beverly

Hills boutique, Judith Brewer made custom-cut "fur" coats from shredded white paper for $200. "I made them just the way I used to make pom-poms," she explained. It couldn't be cleaned; owners were advised to snip off the dirty parts.

The Joseph Magnin Co. opened News Stand boutiques in its 28 stores to carry the paper dresses. Abraham & Strauss had their Wastepaper Basket Boutique. Industrial designer Inman Cook planned to open Paperworks in Manhattan to sell not only paper clothes, but paper furnishings for the home including curtains, drapes, tablecloths and sheets.

A charity ball at the Wadsworth Atheneum in Hartford, Connecticut, asked all 150 women attending to dress in paper, and the event was covered by *The New York Times.* Many of the gowns were worked up for the occasion by top designers, including Bill Blass, Tzaims Luksus, Rudi Gernreich and Peter Max. One of the men wore a paper cumberbund and another claimed to have on disposable underwear in keeping with the spirit.

Among other trend-setters spotted in paper dresses were the Duchess of Windsor, Joan Kennedy, Claudia Cardinale, and Princess Lee Radziwell. The Beatles even sported neon-orange paper jackets during a visit to Los Angeles.

Kimberly-Stevens' Kaycel, a blend of 93 percent cellulose and 7 percent cotton, was the material of choice for these creations. When the manufacturer could not keep up with the demand, DuPont's Reemay and Kendall's Webril filled in.

With 60 clothing manufacturers producing paper clothing, the fashion industry was sure that the future belonged to disposables. Kaycel marketing experts figured on selling $50 million worth of their product that year, and expected the figure to reach $300 million annually by 1972. "Paper clothing, apparently, is here to stay," announced *Time* magazine in 1967. Ronald Bard, sales vice president of Mars Manufacturing Company predicted that "Within ten years most of the world will go disposable."

Fortunately for our over-stuffed landfills, it never happened. The paper dress turned out to be a passing fad rather than a permanent fixture on the fashion scene. Even with all the heady predictions, designers had noted problems. "Paper needs a new architecture," said one. "It doesn't stabilize on you like cloth." The nature of paper was such that it tended to balloon out in all the wrong places. Outside of disposable hospital garb, paper clothing is yesterday's news.

PARFUM BIC

Parfum BIC was "the world's first fine French perfume that combined high quality with affordable pricing and stylish portable design," read the promotional copy. It was to be the perfume that "puts Paris in your pocket," according to the ads.

In 1989, the BIC Corp. attempted to market the fragrances through the drug stores, mass merchandisers, supermarkets and convenience stores that handle its disposable lighters, shavers, and ballpoint pens.

After considerable promotion, BIC withdrew the line the following year, taking an $11 million loss. The problem? According to marketing experts, fragrance is an emotional sell to women. But Parfum BIC did not tug at their subliminal strings with images of glamor, allure and sophistication. The $5 glass flask of Parfum BIC looked pretty much like a 79-cent BIC lighter. *Eau de Butane!*

PERFUME CONCERT

Sixty years before Hollywood came up with AromaRama, a vaudeville performer named Sadakichi Hartmann had already proved that audiences would hate the concept. Billing himself as a "Japanese-German inventor," his act provided a hint of the potential for mischief in that union. Using a battery of electric fans aimed at his audience, Hartmann assaulted their nostrils with billowing clouds of scented smoke in what he called "perfume concerts." The performance had an international flair, with Hartmann explaining in his fractured English which nation each different scent represented: roses for England, violets for Germany, etc. He didn't require a large repertoire as it never took long before he was booed off the stage.

PET PRODUCTS

- In 1956, Bertha Dlugi patented the bird diaper, so owners of canaries and parkeets would no longer have to deal with the tray at the bottom of the cage, not to mention the droppings that inevitably hit the floor beneath it. The bird diaper is held on by straps that pass around the tail, between the legs, and clasp to a collar around the bird's neck. It does not interfere with the bird's normal hopping or flying. It would be available in different sizes, of course.
- French's People Crackers for Dogs were packaged

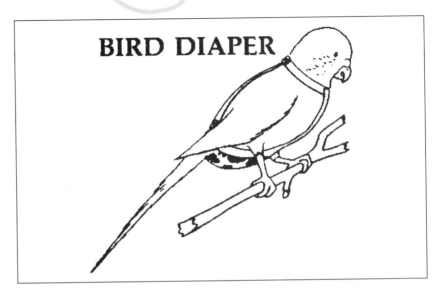

BIRD DIAPER

to resemble the traditional animal crackers, only with people for your dog to bite. These people included "crunchy little milkmen, mailmen, policemen, dog catchers, and burglars."

- Down the pet food memory hole went Purina Homestyle ("the quick dog dinner that's like home-made") and Baker Tom's Baked Cat Food. Then there's Goff's Low Ash Cat Food ("contains only 1.5 percent ash"). Why make "Low Ash" content a selling point when most people don't know that cat food has any ash at all? Even the kitty on the label looks upset, as if she, too, just got the news.

- For those motorcyclists whose dogs liked to ride behind them, motoring goggles for dogs were available for $7.50 in the 1960s.

- Doggie Dent was a beef-flavored toothpaste developed especially for dogs by Ursula Dietrich, a California dentist. If that didn't do the trick, a company once offered Happy Breath, a breath-freshening spray for dogs.

- For a more dignified send-off than the traditional flush down the toilet, the Bird and Small Animal Burial Kit was created. It included a small, mahogany-colored plastic coffin with a lid and green-flocked lining, and a marbleized plastic headstone.

- While on the topic of matters religious, DuSay's, a New Orleans specialty shop, offered yarmulkes for dogs. Rover's skullcap is in perfect taste, white with a blue Star of David, held on with a chin strap and priced at $2.98.
- What dog wouldn't be proud to have his treats kept in his own gold and rhinestone cookie jar, with a picture of his breed laminated into the front and the legend, "My Favorite Yummy"?
- Parfumes do Poodle-oo was a dog perfume that came in two scents—Le Chien No. 5 and Arf-peg-gio. And it's not the only such venture. Donna Douglas, the actress who played Elly Mae Clampett on The Beverly Hillbillies, invented Critter Country Classics pet cologne. There was Miss Tabby for cats and Timber Wolf for dogs.
- Not a best-seller was 1963's The Secret of Cooking for Dogs.
- In 1978, a Virginia firm introduced "Solar Rover." It was a solar-heated dog house, storing heat during the day and releasing it at night to keep Rover warm. Faced with the $800 cost, most people fig-ured Rover could rough it.
- The Natural Method of Dog Training, a 1968 man-ual, suggests you starve your dog in order to teach it tricks, cover furniture with carpet tacks to keep your dog from jumping on it, set rat traps in the garden to discourage your dog from digging in it, and throw firecrackers at your dog to teach him not to chase cars.
- In the 1990s, a twenty-five minute video tape was produced for your dog's entertainment by Made-For-Dog-Video. It was shot from a dog's point of view, about two feet off the ground, and featured a car ride, a duck chase, a visit to the pet store and a cow round-up. It was advertised as "a tape your dog can watch over and over again."

PICTUREPHONE

It is surprising how many 1960s predictions about the future of the telephone were accurate. Speed dialing, call waiting, call forwarding, conference calling, car phones, portable wallet-sized phones and laser transmission of sound have all come to pass. But the one we all remember is the one that never materialized.

In early 1964, with considerable fanfare, AT&T unveiled its latest communications breakthrough at the 1964 World's Fair in New York. It was the Picturephone, the "see-as-you-talk phone." There was a demonstration hook-up between the World's Fair and Disneyland, but AT&T promised that connections would soon be available in three major cities. Those who wished to use the service would have to make their arrangements by regular old phones in advance, then each would have to go to the proper location in his city: in New York City, Grand Central Station; in Chicago, the Prudential Insurance Company; in Washington, D.C., the National Geographic Society Building. Rates would be expensive. A three-minute call between Washington and Chicago that would normally run $1.35 would cost $21 by Picturephone. This expense was due to the fact that, while the regular telephone used only one circuit, the Picturephone required the equivalent of 125 of them, for the 125 lines on its 4-by-5-inch video screen. As *Time* magazine put it in its 1964 feature on Ma Bell, "With confidence that this problem will be solved, AT&T sees a bright and profitable future for its latest device."

An example AT&T gave of the Picturephone's value was to the hat designer who wanted to show his new collection to buyers. Instead of having to describe his ideas, he could hold them up and display them. The communication time would be reduced from an hour to a moment. Perhaps there just weren't enough hat designers around; the cost of Picturephone service proved to be higher than anyone was willing to pay. It did enjoy interoffice use within the Bell System itself.

Bell dusted off the Picturephone concept again in

1970, once again confidently predicting success. 100,000 units were to be sold or leased by 1975, and the system was projected to be "widely used by the general public" by the 1980s. Once again, there was little serious interest.

The 1980s saw sneak attacks on AT&T's territory by Sony and Mitsubishi. Their video telephones could only send black-and-white still images, and conversation had to be suspended during the transmission. Why bother? The decade saw videoconferencing become a part of corporate culture, but it required specialized networks and expensive equipment (about $25,000 worth).

In 1992, AT&T introduced the VideoPhone 2500, an old dog with some new tricks. Looking like an ordinary business telephone, it features a flip-up 2-by-2 1/2-inch color video screen. The difficulty in transmitting moving images had always been the tremendous volume of information that had to be sent over a single wire, comparable to trying to channel a river through a garden hose. The solution came with the development of "signal compression," which reduces the video's 92 million bits per second to a manageable 19 thousand, then "reconstitutes" them at the receiving end. At this time, unfortunately, the single line makes it impossible to get high video quality; at ten frames a second, the movement was remniscent of early silent movies. Add to that the fact that the picture trailed the sound, and your party looked like he had a speaking part in a *Godzilla* movie. Since the VideoPhone transmits over a single telephone line the call is no more costly than usual, but the unit itself is a hefty $1,500. Whether it joins the long line of previous flops remains to be seen.

The video telephone has been a perennial fixture in science fiction films, probably because it's a cheap special effect, looks advanced, and is a useful story-telling device. Nevertheless, for those of us who've grown up watching *Star Trek*, it's hard to picture the future without it. Perhaps the same sci-fi inspired assumption drives AT&T to try to force this technology upon the public: "It'll never be the future until we have Picturephones!" AT&T claims that marketing surveys continue to demonstrate that interest in the technology is "intense." As in every other poll or survey, one wonders who they've been talking to. As a means of communication the telephone, like the radio, does not need pictures. Its combination of intimacy and anonymity is fine the way it is. What most of us want from our phones is portability above all else, and the Picturephone would require that we plant ourselves in front of a sending-and-receiving apparatus. And anyway, do you really want the boss to get a good look at you when you're calling in sick?

PNEUMATIC SUBWAY

By the 1860s, New York streets were clogged with horse-drawn carriages, omnibuses and freight wagons. The inability to travel quickly throughout the city seemed to restrict any further growth. In 1863, the first subway went into service in London. Though the service was dirty and dangerous, with coal-burning engines spewing fumes into the underground tunnels, New Yorkers were nonetheless envious.

Alfred Eli Beach, inventor and publisher of *Scientific American*, became obsessed with building a subway for New York that would avoid the problems of the London system. He decided upon a subway that would operate pneumatically, having already invented the pneumatic tube as a way of delivering mail, a system which is still used in some offices and at the drive-in windows of banks. At the 1863 Fair of the American Institute in New York City, he exhibited a system by which a ten-passenger car was driven through a tube by a powerful fan. When it came to building the real thing, though, he encountered opposition from Boss Tweed, the crooked political boss of New York. In 1868, Beach obtained a permit to construct a large-sized underground pneumatic mail tube as a cover for his real plan: to build a full-sized working prototype of his subway. For two years his workers burrowed secretly

OPENING OF THE BROADWAY TUNNEL IN NEW YORK

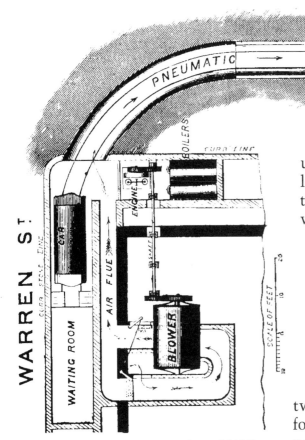

The tunnel under Broadway [1870]

under congested Broadway at the lower end of Manhattan. They started their tunnel through the basement wall of Devlin's clothing store, and worked only at night. They smuggled the dirt out like the POWs in *The Great Escape*. On February 28, 1870, Beach opened the doors of his system, only 312-feet long. The station was opulent, with wall frescoes, a fountain, even a grand piano. A 100-horsepower fan at one end, alternately blowing and sucking, moved the twenty-two passenger car back and forth through the 8-foot diameter tunnel. One passenger praised the ride as "so smooth it was like being sucked through a straw and then blown back again."

The project was never developed further due to the continuing opposition of Boss Tweed, the financial panic of 1873, and the introduction of electric engines. It closed down in 1873.

POLAVISION, SPECTRAVISION, AND BETA

In the late 1970s and early 1980s, Polaroid and RCA introduced new products to the home entertainment market. Both had every reason to expect that their massive investments in research and development would be rewarded. Neither could have known that they would soon be roadkill, flattened by the technological juggernaut that dominated consumer electronics in the 1980s—the VCR.

At the annual Polaroid stockholder's meeting in April, 1977, Edwin Land, the wizard behind the instant camera, proudly unveiled his latest brainchild—the movie-in-a-minute Polavision camera. Land pronounced it the "new way to relate oneself to life," and said "It will become part of your diary."

Despite Polaroid's confidence the system had a few flaws, among them its grainy picture, no sound, 2 1/2 minute cassettes that sold for $9.95 each, and a camera that carried a list price of $675. Moreover, to view the cassette it had to be inserted into a special television-style viewer, which processed the film, rewound and played it.

There was no way Polavision could compete with the video systems then coming onto the market. Dealers who carried Polavision found it impossible to move by 1979. "This is the all-time turkey," griped the manager of a large photo-products store in Chicago. "It's a real dud." Marvin Saffian, an industry analyst, said "Polavision is just the wrong product for the wrong market at the wrong time."

The company insisted that the verdict was not yet in on its new technology, and that Polaroid had a history of making short term losers into eventual winners. "The newer, more innovative a product, the greater the difficulty in finding the way to sell it," said the senior vice president for marketing. Among the straws grasped at was the fact that the U.S. Olympic ski team used Polavision as their official camera to track downhill racers. That made sense—any skiier who hadn't made it down by the time the 2 1/2 minute tape ran out should be cut from the team anyway. Golf and tennis pros were also cited among those who could use it as a teaching tool. And there was medical endoscopy—the visual examination of internal organs. Not exactly a large market from which to recoup an investment of $100 million, but it was a start. Land was known for his dedication to his own inventions, and analyst Saffian described his support for Polavision as "sort of a holy crusade;" like the Crusades, it too was a costly, drawn-out failure. In 1979, Polaroid cancelled it, writing-off $68 million in Polavision losses.

The same sad fate awaited RCA's SelectaVision. This mechanical marvel took Edison's basic phonograph record and managed to store pictures on it as well as sound, stretching the envelope of 19th century technology. While others were exploiting the potential of the laser, SelectaVision used a diamond-tipped stylus traveling through the microscopic grooves of a prerecorded disc. The ten-year development of the videodisc player had been conducted in such secrecy that the company dubbed it the Manhattan Project, the code name under which the atomic bomb was developed. In 1981 RCA was ready to market the result. Its $20 million ad campaign claimed that it was "introducing the most exciting new form of entertainment since television." It expected to sell 500,000 videodisc players in its first year, and predicted that it would be a $7.5 billion market by 1990, with pre-recorded discs bringing in an additional $200 to $250 million annually. In fact, no more than 80,000 of RCA's videodisc players were sold in 1981, and its high point was 1983, when it moved 250,000. SelectaVision suffered partly from confusion with Magnavox's Magnavision and Pioneer's LaserDisc, two incompatible (and superior) technologies. RCA figured it could outdo these competitors on price, ease of operation and the number of titles available in its format; it even thought it could compete with the VCR on these points. It just happened to be wrong. An adequate library was not available for the SelectaVision at the time that the mass of consumers was making its decision about which system to choose, and it was hard to get people to buy a machine that could play but not record when they could have one that did both. RCA cancelled SelectaVision in 1984, having lost a spectacular $580 million on the system. Like the original Manhattan Project, it had created a truly stupendous bomb.

By the early 1990s, eighty percent of all American households owned at least one VCR, and the sale and rental of tapes was an $11 billion business. RCA had been right about the market, but wrong about the technology that would capture it.

The last great battle of the video wars was fought between Sony's 1/3-inch Betamax system and the 1/2-inch VHS format. Sony was first on the field with its one-hour format. Matsushita/JVC, Mitsubishi, and Hitachi soon came out with the VHS system that offered two-hour cassettes. Sony came out with Beta 2, a two-hour cassette, but to the consumers' annoyance, it was incompatible with the original system. With its longer tapes, and the backing of RCA's distribution system, the tide turned in favor of VHS. Consumers rushed to join the winning side. Throughout the eighties the battle could be

witnessed at video rental stores where Beta's shelf space, once equal to that of VHS, was slowly surrendered, finally disappearing entirely. Sony still produces the machine, and Beta has its partisans who claim it gives a better picture. Like the Chinese Nationalist Army holed up on Taiwan, refusing to concede defeat, they must take their satisfaction from symbolic victories. One was Disney's recent decision to release *Snow White* in their favored format.

POLYFIDELITY

In many ways the Kerista Commune was like any number of other utopian experiments. It was founded in San Francisco in 1971. Members lived together in one of several houses that they communally owned, and could work in the group's business, in this case a thriving computer service. Profits were returned to the business, as members were not supposed to accumulate money. All property was shared, from cars to clothing. Names were dropped in favor of short, cute nicknames—Sun, Eve, Laf, Keg, Now, Jaz, etc. But beyond this unexceptional behavior, the Keristas were organized around a complex, central theory called Polyfidelity. They regarded it as a major breakthrough in the organization of family structure, one which would come to change the way human life is lived.

Polyfidelity was a group marriage between an equal number of men and women, with a total number of 36 being considered optimal. Within the group, or B-FIC (Best Friend Identity Cluster), each of the women had a sexual relationship with each of the men in a non-preferential manner. This was ensured by the "Balanced Rotational Sleeping Schedule." The B-FIC women's names were written on a wheel, which rotated within a larger wheel on which the men's names were written. Each day the wheel moved ahead a single turn, and those two members paired off for the night, over and over again. No sex was allowed outside of the group. To quote from a Kerista publication, *The Blueprint for Heaven on Earth*, "old fashioned romantics might consider such a system too 'mechanical,' but those who use it think it's a marvelous way to ensure that every twosome [or "dyad"] in a B-FIC has equal and ample time to build their own special, one-to-one intimacy." Every such dyad was acknowledged to have its own unique qualities (called "lovjoy"), but any preference for one particular partner within the B-FIC was strictly *verboten*. Polyfidelity was thought to be the answer to the human desire for sexual variety, within the context of lasting, permanent relationships. Admission to a B-FIC was a serious matter, and applicants had to be considered long and hard. Considerations based on racism, classism and ageism were ruled out, though members tended to be white, middle-class, well-educated, and—with the exception of Jud, the Jerry Garcia-ish founder and patriarch—youthful and slim. Other obvious prerequisites were a horny attitude and a high tolerance for jargon. The admission ceremony was called "stepping over the broom," and

...PREPARING THEM TO SHIFT UP TO THE NEXT GROWTH STAGE, FROM THEIR SEED NUCLEUS GROUP TO A FULL-SCALE HEAVEN-ON-EARTH PROTOTYPE MODEL. AT THAT STAGE, THEIR ENERGY LEVEL WILL BE STUPENDOUS, ARTISTICALLY, PHILANTHROPICALLY AND EVERY WAY.

MAKES PERFECT SENSE.

**THE BALANCED ROTATIONAL
SLEEPING SCHEDULE**

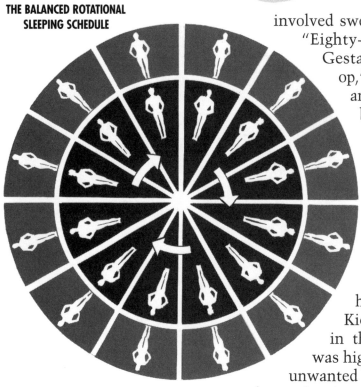

involved swearing alignment with the "Eighty-Eight Standards of the Gestalt-O-Rama Growth Co-op," receiving a special name, and ritualistically crossing a broom laid north-to-south on the floor. The inductee went several times around the sleeping cycle without any physical intimacies in order to receive final approval, and to await the results of VD and AIDS tests. Within a year, all males had to have vasectomies. Kids were a definite turn-off in the Kerista lifestyle; there was high-minded talk of adopting unwanted babies at some time in the future, but it never happened.

Naturally, there were difficulties in managing this large group marriage, which were hashed out at regular evening "Gestalt-O-Rama" sessions, a combination of encounter group and brainwashing (if you believe there's any difference between those two). Those put on the "hot seat" were subjected to examinations that could last long into the night. Though the group on the surface was resolutely democratic and feminist it was always dominated by Jud, who had the advantage of being well-rested for late-night meetings, as he slept all day. Judgments were rendered on the basis of the "88 Basic Standards," such rules as:

#15. Graceful Distancing. Any disengagement from a previous involvement is expected to be graceful, i.e., without ill will.

#29. Hold Your Own Mud. Do not dump personal disturbances on anyone else.

#41. Positive Attitude Toward the Toggle Switch Mode of Decision Making. Basic choices should be made in a straight-forward manner, without vagueness or indecision.

#87. Keeping Up With Turns. The ability to keep up with the latest twist and turns in group thinking, and by golly there were many. For example, for a long time it was forbidden for members to hate anything, until in a doctrinal shift it was decided that it was all right to hate hateful stuff like war and racism.

All this got very complicated and doctrinaire, as you might have noticed, and we're not even getting into their theories about ouija boards and Joan Jett. What is interesting is that the Keristans thought that polyfidelity was a breakthrough discovery that would revolutionize society. They were the trail-blazers of a whole new order, astronauts in the cosmic consciousness. They propounded their theory in a gush of publications, including a series of comic strips featuring scenes of Polyfidelistas strolling sylvan glades or lounging nude in a hot tub while discoursing in didactic, over-stuffed word balloons. (The Kersitans spent so much time hashing out and proselytizing Polyfidelity that it's a wonder they had energy left to practice it.) They reasoned that if only 36 out of a thousand people adopted the Kerista lifestyle, that would amount to 10,080,000 in North America alone. Since living communally is more efficient than living separately, they figured this would free up $115 billion to be applied to solving the world's problems. All that would be required to get the process going, they reasoned, was one perfectly-functioning group of 36. After the prototype was perfected, it would be a simple matter to replicate its structure with other groups—much as computer software, once developed, can run any number of separate systems.

The problem was in developing that first perfect B-FIC, which never quite happened. Membership got as high as twenty-eight for the main cluster, but members were continually splitting off into smaller groups, an accepted process called "divide and regroup;" or (heresy!) pairing off and leaving the group entirely. Even this self-selected group in this largely self-selected city could not make the theory work. The thought that Polyfidelity would ever have caught on in El Salvador or Suriname, two fertile terrritiories suggested in the literature, seems a tad whimsical.

Citing irreconcilable differences, the Kerista Commune broke up in the early 1990s. It was a messy divorce.

PREMATURE BURIAL ALARM

Count Karnice Karnicki, a Russian nobleman, claimed to have been at the funeral of a young girl who awoke in her coffin when the first shovelfuls of dirt were thrown upon it. Traumatized by her screams, he set about inventing a device that would avert the ghastly tragedy that might have followed, and in 1901 patented the Premature Burial Alarm. The buried coffin would be connected to the surface with a six-foot length of pipe.

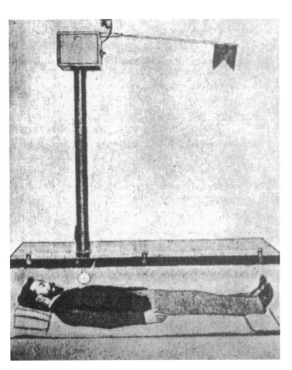
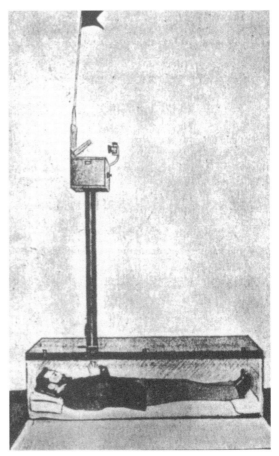

Atop the pipe was a hermetically-sealed box, which would prevent gases from escaping the coffin in the event that the occupant was, in fact, dead. On the chest of the alleged corpse would rest a glass ball connected through the pipe to the box by cable. Should the ball move, disturbed by the breathing of the coffin's occupant, it would trigger the box on the surface. Immediately, its top would spring open, admitting air and light to the coffin. At the same time a four-foot-high, spring-loaded flag would pop up and a bell would ring for a half hour. An electric light would continue to provide illumination underground after sunset. The prematurely-buried party could speak through the pipe to his rescuers.

Count Karnicki's invention was only one of a number of similar designs to be patented. (There was also a less sentimental approach—a coffin whose closing lid broke vials of cyanide gas to ensure that the dearly departed didn't get any funny ideas.) It was tested and worked just fine, but evidently fear of premature burial was not sufficiently widespread to justify its manufacture. Considering the lengths to which funeral directors will go to part mourners from their money, this must have been a disappointment.

QUESTIONABLE MEDICAL DEVICES

The Museum of Questionable Medical Devices in Minneapolis boasts the world's largest display of quackish contraptions, with some 432 on display. Its curator, Bob McCoy, has appeared on *The David Letterman Show*, *Good Morning America*, *Today*, and the *Tonight Show* with Johnny Carson to demonstrate the devices he has collected over the past thirty years. He doesn't need any kind of medical license in order to do so, as he guarantees everything not to work. He also addresses medical groups on the topic of health fraud. McCoy, a dead ringer for W.C. Fields, seems an ideal figure to discourse on the cure-alls whose motto seems to be: "Never give a sucker an even break." Among the items in his museum:

- The 1905 Psycograph brought scientific precision to a fortune-telling art normally performed with the fingers. A wire-festooned helmet fits over the head like an old-fashioned hair dryer. The thirty-two sensitive measuring devices—one for each of the 32 mental faculties represented by the bumps on the skull—are able to provide a printed-out personality profile, quantifying dignity, wit, and individuality, as well as "sublimity," "alimentiveness," and "sexamity." It even offers career guidance, suggesting vocations from "insurance salesman" to "zeppelin attendant." Incidentally, after his death Franz Gall, the father of the science of phrenology, was found to have a skull of twice the normal thickness.

- The Foot-Operated Breast Enlarger Pump was advertised on late-night TV in 1976, and sold four million units at $9.95. Those desiring the treatment fit suction cups over their breasts and created a vacuum in them with a foot-pump. Says McCoy, "There were three cup sizes—large, larger and even larger." Unfortunately, all the machine could produce was a giant, painful hickey. Men fell prey to similar pitches, investing their hopes and dreams in the Vital Power Vacuum Massager, the "perfect organ developing appliance."

- Also for men was the G-H-R Electric Thermitis Dilator from 1918. The foot-long device was designed to be plugged into an electrical socket at one end and a man's rectum at the other. Once in place, it would heat to more than 100 degrees, stimulating the prostate gland, or "the so-called abdominal brain," as its literature mysteriously describes it. With regular treatments, the device promised to restore the user's sex drive. "I'd rather be a monk," says McCoy.

- The Electric Thermitis Dilator didn't do the trick? You still suffer from "glandular fatigue," and are unable "to joyfully meet the duties and opportuni-

Antique Phrenology Machine — 1905

ties" that come to you? Try the Testone Radium Energizer and Suspensory. Yes, in 1930 a radium-impregnated jock strap was available from the Home Products Company of Denver, Colorado, delivered to your door in a plain wrapper. As the brochure says, "Soon after fastening this wonderful Testone Radium Appliance in position, you should feel the warmth in the genital organs" which will

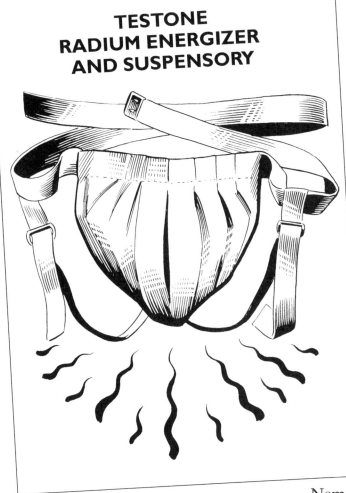

**TESTONE
RADIUM ENERGIZER
AND SUSPENSORY**

let you know it's "toning up and strengthening those weakened glands and cords." Not to mention that seductive glow-in-the-dark effect.

Many of the best-selling quack devices relate in some way to sex, as those too embarrassed to talk to their doctor about sexual problems sought relief through mail order.

From 1920 there's the Spectro-Chrome, which used colored lights to cure cancer. From the same decade, the Omnipotent Oscilloclast identified illnesses from the "vibration rate" of blood samples. The Homo-Vibra Ray Instrument was a diagnosis device of dubious merit, and the electrically-powered Nemectron claimed to "normalize" the breasts, making them larger or smaller as necessary. The Polizer of 1957 was a mercury-filled glass tube which "pol-ized" the oxygen in drinking water, curing arthritis, diabetes and constipation. It could also make bad wine taste good. (Especially if some of that yummy mercury leaked out.) "The Toftness Radiation Detector of 1988, a contraption fashioned out of PVC pipe, claimed to "draw noxious energy from the body." Many were sold to chiropractors at $2,400 apiece.

Though the items in The Museum of Medical Devices seem comically unworkable, McCoy reminds us that the gullible still fall prey to bunko artists when hope overwhelms reason. Steve McQueen traveled to Mexico for coffee enemas to cure his cancer, and Michael Jackson allegedly sleeps in a hyperbaric chamber to slow the aging process. And at rave parties, the trendoids drink amino acid cocktails that are supposed to make them smarter. How smart do they get? Not smart enough, apparently.

RABAGE

In 1924 a Soviet geneticist named Karpenchenko created the *Rephanobrassica*, or rabage. It was a combination of those two great staples of the Russian diet, the cabbage and the radish, hearty vegetables which grew despite the most indifferent efforts of collective farmers. It was intended to produce a plump, edible root with a tasty, leafy head and since it produced seeds it was capable of enduring as a new species. Unfortunately, Karpenchenko was not destined to become a Hero of Soviet Agriculture. Despite all efforts at selective breeding, the rabage refused to produce anything but the thin, inedible greens of a radish atop the small, useless root of a cabbage.

RECORDS, WRETCHED

Albums that never made the hit parade:

Ali and His Gang Vs. Mr. Tooth Decay: A Children's Story, by Muhammad Ali with Frank Sinatra, Richie Havens, Jayne Kennedy and others, including "special announcer Howard Cosell." Produced by Arthur Bernard Morrison. It was titled "Volume 1," though it's hard to believe The Greatest could require more than one LP to knock-out Mr. Tooth Decay. Perhaps further bouts had been set up with Mr. Foot Odor, Mr. Acne and Mr. Unsightly Dandruff.

American Gun Album: A Celebration in Song (sold only on late night television).

A country music album with song titles familiar from bumper stickers, such as "I'd Rather be Tried by Twelve (than Carried by Six)," "If Guns Are Outlawed, Only Outlaws Will Have Guns," "Never Mind the Dog—Beware of Owner." Came with free oiled plastic rifle case. Next time you hear a bump in the night, throw this on the turntable.

Arnold Palmer's Music for Swinging Golfers, Mark 56.

Granny's Mini-Skirt by Irene Ryan, Nashwood, 1965. Granny of *The Beverly Hillbillies* sings lyrics such as "When I do the twist and jerk/ It drives old grandpa wild." Forgive me for putting that image in your head.

If The Bomb Falls, Tops Records, 1961. "A Recorded Guide to Survival" in the event of nuclear war, with Civil Defense guides enclosed. The cover features a mushroom cloud and various fear-mongering newspaper articles. Better hope you get at least 45 minutes advance warning, 'cause it's an LP.

Joey Bishop Sings Country Western, ABC, 1968. The Borscht Belt comic, failed late night talk show host, and minor member of Frank Sinatra's Rat Pack tries his pipes on Hank Williams' classics.

Music to be Murdered By, by Alfred Hitchcock, Imperial Records. Instrumentals with Hitch introducing each track in his inimitable manner. Example: "Why shouldn't I make a record? After all, my measurements are 33-45-78!"

Music To Make Automobiles By..., Volkswagen of America.

Music to Relax By In Your Barcalounger, Columbia Records. The collection of easy listening features a suburban couple on the cover, dressed as if for a night on the town, each blissfully reclining in their own Barcalounger.

Sebastian Cabot, actor. Bob Dylan, poet. a dramatic reading with music, MGM, 1967. The portly actor who played Mr. French on TV's *Family Affair* emotes the work of Bob Dylan. This may be what drove one of his former charges to hold up a convenience store.

Shakespeare, Tchaikovsky and Me, by Jayne Mansfield, MGM Records. The abundantly-talented actress breathily whispers poetry by Shakespeare, Byron, Shelley, Browning, Yeats, Dryden and Suckling (yes, look it up) while someone tinkles out Tchaikovsky on the piano. The album's cover features Mansfield clutching a mink stole over her swelling bosom. Her lips are pursed as she looks sideways at plaster busts of the Dead White European Males. I'd take this over George McGovern's LP from Spoken Arts, Inc., in which he drones out the inaugural addresses of Washington, Lincoln, Jefferson, and Theodore Roosevelt.

Sound Effects U. S. Air Force Firepower, Audio Fidelity. Includes the sound of a sonic boom, strafing runs, firing mixed loads of rockets at ground targets, 20mm. Vulcan gatling gun, mass napalm attack, B-52 taxiing, nuclear bomb explosion (Yucca Flat, Nevada) etc. Got the woofers for this one?

Spectacular Accordians by Charles Camilleri, MGM Records. "Dramatic effects—thrilling realism—unforgettable listening!" the subtitle explains, and who could doubt it? The cover shows a woman in a yellow leotard, who appears to be enjoying herself perched atop one of three giant accordions.

This Time by Richard Simmons, Elektra, 1982. The insufferable exercise guru's attempt at a hit single. Did not reach the charts in any market.

Transformed Man, by William Shatner, Decca, 1966. Among other atrocities on this album, Shatner pulls out all the stops in his rendition of Dylan's *Mr. Tamborine Man*. According to rock critics Jimmy Guterman and Owen O'Donnell, "He invests each line with either significantly more or less emotion than is called for, and he occasionally puts emphasis on the wrong word in the sentence or pauses at the wrong spot to make it clear that he has no idea what he is doing... He screams louder and louder after the song is supposed to end, like a kid running after an ice cream truck, finally screeching the song's title *a capella* after the studio musicians have wisely packed up their instruments and left..."

Two Sides of Leonard Nimoy, by Leonard Nimoy. One side of the album features the actor singing tunes such as "Gentle On My Mind" and "The Ballad of Bilbo Baggins", the other his Mr. Spock persona performing such numbers as "Highly Illogical", about the contradictions of the human race.

Where Did You Come From? by Art Linkletter, 20th Century Fox. A 1963 record on which the cloying television host explains the facts of life using animal analogies: "the small tube at the bottom of the daddy horse inserts his sperm into the egg..." If Mr. Linkletter calls that a small tube, he's got more going for him than anyone suspected.

You're My Girl, romantic reflections by Jack Webb, Warner Bros. Records. Jack Webb, Sgt. Joe Friday of *Dragnet* fame, addresses matters of love in his terse, nasal, no-nonsense monotone.

REGGIE!

The Baby Ruth was not named after the Sultan of Swat, as many believe, but after the daughter of Grover Cleveland; the Reggie! was the first candy bar named after a baseball player.

The notoriously free-spending CEO of Standard Brands, F. Ross Johnson, loved sports and enjoyed schmoozing with professional athletes. One of the ways to win their friendship was to sign them up for lucrative promotional deals, of course. In 1978 he signed up Reggie Jackson of the N.Y. Yankees to lend his name and image to the round chocolate-covered caramel and peanut patty. The wrapper had a picture of Jackson batting. Reggie! bars were handed out to everyone entering Yankee Stadium on opening day that year, and when

Jackson hit a home run they would rain down onto the field. Unlike its namesake, though, the Reggie! wasn't a superstar, and in 1980 it was cut from the lineup. Reggie himself was not, however. For several years afterward Johnson authorized an annual personal-services fee of $400,000, plus a company apartment and car. Hey, what're friends for?

ROCKET BELT

If you didn't happen to be born on the planet Krypton, this was as good as it could get. With a backpack sprouting twin jets, you could fly across rivers or up to the top of a three-story building, at speeds of up to thirty miles per hour. A motorcycle-type twist grip on the right controlled the rate of climb and descent, and a steering stick on the left controlled the yaw, or sideways direction.

Officially called the SRLD (for Small Rocket Lift Device), the rocket belt was developed at the Bell Aerosystems Laboratory by Wendell Moore, and demonstrated to the public in 1961. When the pilot opened the throttle, pressurized hydrogen peroxide was released into a gas generator, where contact with a catalytic agent broke it down into steam. The steam jetting out through the nozzles at either side provided lift. The nozzles where set out far enough, and exhaust temperatures were low enough, to eliminate the need for special protective clothing. The propulsion system weighed over a hundred pounds, and was mounted to a fiberglass "corset" molded to fit the individual pilot and held fast by a safety belt. Unlike Superman or Buck Rogers, he flew in an upright position.

The original hope was to sell the SRLD to the Army, which helped fund the research. Troops in amphibious landings could use it to rocket across the water to the beach. Cliffs and hills could be easily surmounted. Creeks and rivers, deep ravines, barbed wire obstructions and minefields would pose no obstacle to the rocket-powered GI of the future. In one demonstration during maneuvers at Fort Bragg, a Bell pilot dressed in fatigues flew across a pond, his jets kicking up a ferocious spray, landed and saluted an impressed President Kennedy. The rocket belt was even rigged to fire a couple of small missiles, though no one was ever able to hit anything with them.

Bell saw wider application for its SRLD technology. In promotional films, a rocketeer lays a telephone cable over difficult terrain, and drops off a lifesaver to a drowning

swimmer. The film makes the whole procedure look effortlessly precise and unbelievably fun. A pair of rocket belt-wearers is shown taking a leisurely flight over a wilderness area, swooping down to slalom between tall pines. As the film implies, Bell hoped that the rocket belt would become a popular recreational item, like jet-skis and dirt bikes have become.

The problems with the rocket belt did not show up on the film. For one thing, the soundtrack dampened its ongodly din. Also, to get the effect of soaring for long distances it was necessary to splice together clips of many different flights, each of which was in fact quite short. The rocket belt only held 21 seconds of fuel and had never gone farther than 360 feet. A vibrating device on the back of the pilot's helmet warned him when fuel was low, but once it ran out the only further travel was straight down. Most of the time, pilots flew only a few feet off the ground.

The SRLD was also extremely difficult to use. The slightest body movement could easily send it out of control. Only a few experts were ever allowed to demonstrate the device. Bill Suter and Harry Graham are the only two I've seen mentioned. Suter flew a newer, pulse-jet version at the opening ceremonies of the 1984 Olympics at Los Angeles. Graham (who articles always mentioned was a bachelor, as if to allay in advance concerns about a grieving widow), described flying it as "like having a big person...a giant...pick you up by your arms." And if you're not careful, throw you back down on the ground, hard.

THE SAN FRANCISCO SOUND, FORGOTTEN BANDS OF

The San Francisco Sound was more of a social than a musical phenomenon. It brought a number of innovations to the music scene, including rock poster art, light shows, higher production values in concert performances, better recording contracts for musicians, the establishment of a serious rock journalism with

Rolling Stone, etc. It also pioneered really bizarre names for bands, unmatched until the advent of punk rock. *The Strawberry Alarm Clock* and *The Peanut Butter Conspiracy* were among the psychedelic bands that made it big, albeit briefly. The following ones, from a list rock journalist Ralph Gleason compiled in 1968, did not. Was it the names?

A Cid Symphony
Amplified Ohm
Ballpoint Banana
Black Shit Puppy Farm
Blue Crumb Truck Factory
Celestial Hysteria
Chocolate Watchband
Cleanliness and Godliness Skiffle Band
Colossal Pomegranate
Evergreen Tangerine
Fifty-Foot Hose
Immaculate Contraption
Magnesium Water Lily
Melvin Q. Watchpocket
Mysore Sugoundhi Dhoop Factory
The Only Alternative and His Other Possibilities
William Penn and His Pals
Pipe Joint Compound
Rhythm Method Blues Band
Truman Coyote

SIMPLIFIED SPELLING BOARD

The late nineteenth century gave birth to a multitude of progressive social movements, from women's suffrage, to child labor laws, to temperance. Somewhat lost in the shuffle was the Simplified Spelling Board, backed by such estimables as Andrew Carnegie and Theodore Roosevelt. It was founded by Melvil Dewey, developer of the Dewey Decimal system, and Brander Matthews, professor of dramatic literature at Columbia.

George Bernard Shaw, himself an advocate of spelling reform, pointed out that in English, a word spelled *ghoti* could be pronounced "fish"—that's *gh* as in enough, *o* as in women, and *ti* as in nation. The reformers aimed to change this, so that English spelling would be as logical and consistent as that of Italian or Spanish. Their campaign was aimed at converting influential Americans and newspapers to their cause.

Andrew Carnegie backed the movement with a $25,000 annual stipend. Carnegie saw the reforms as central to his pursuit of world peace—he felt that simplified spelling would help make English a universal language, fostering better international communication. In his own writing, Carnegie favored a staccato, telegraphic style, omitting what he regarded as superfluous articles, prepositions, and conjunctions.

The board got a major boost in 1906 when President Theodore Roosevelt signed on. Roosevelt, though a bookish man, may have been the worst speller in American politics till Dan Quayle. Words like "don't" he routinely spelled "do'n't," and in his correspondence he often misspelled the names of his close friends. An additional reason he joined the fight was his violent objection to the insertion of a "u" in words like "colour," "honour," and "parlour"—that was one vestige of British rule he wished to expunge from her former colonies. Roosevelt tried to introduce the spelling reforms in official government documents, and sent his own State of the Union message to Congress in the simplified form. Congress revolted, and adopted a resolution forbidding the printing of public documents in any non-standard orthography. His detractors had a field day with his crusade. An editorial cartoon showed TR, a six-gun in each hand, placing shots into the open spread of a dictionary. Beside him is a box labeled "amunishun." An editorialist for the Louisville *Courier* wrote, "Nothing escapes Mr. Rucevelt. No subject is tu hi for him to takl, nor tu lo for him to notis." Even Mark Twain, himself a somewhat bemused believer in the cause, wrote of his fear that the reform "won't make any hedway. I am as sory as a dog. For I do luv revolutions and violens." Despite his failure to install simplified spelling as the law of the land, Roosevelt continued to use it in his own correspondence, for which he was mercilessly tweaked by his friends.

By 1915, Carnegie had had enough, writing to Henry Holt, then director of the Simplified Spelling Board, "A more useless body of men never came into association, judging from the effects they produced...I think I hav been patient long enuf...I have a much better use for Twenty-five thousand dollars a year." The inconsistencies in the letter illustrate Carnegie's own difficulties with the cause he had espoused. In his correspondence, he often would conscientiously erase "have" and rewrite it with the progressive "hav." Actually, the Simplified Spelling Board effected more real change than the pacifist causes to which Carnegie devoted a large share of his fortune. We still have war, but at least we got the u out of color and no longer spell program "programme."

Simplified spelling suffered from the same inertial resistance that stymied that reform effort of the 1970s—the conversion of America to the metric system. Language fetishists such as William Safire argue that English's archaic spellings and inconsistencies are part of its rich history, and that to tear away that tradition would be to defile our past. So remember that you are honoring your heritage as you recite "i before e, except after c, or when sounded as a, as in neighbor and weigh," and especially when it doesn't, as in leisure and weird.

SKUNKGUARD

Intended to protect women against rapists, Skunkguard brought the defensive technique of the skunk to today's urban jungle. The concentrated, liquid stench of a skunk was packaged in one-inch capsules for $14.95 an ounce. When attacked, a woman was to break the capsule, spreading the *eau de skunk* over herself and her attacker.

Presumably the attacker was then disposed to flee the scene, but the stench clung to him, making it easier for the police to follow and identify him. One man chose Skunkguard for his wife, explaining, "Electrical stingers and Mace often anger attackers and are difficult to use." Evidently he thought that being doused with skunk stench would have a less vexatious effect.

The product worked in theory, though there were no reported cases of its being used. Nevertheless, it sold poorly. The stench came with a neutralizing agent that could remove the scent from skin, but not from clothing, so any clothing doused with Skunkguard would be ruined. This might seem a reasonable trade-off if the product fended off an attacker, but not if the capsule broke accidentally, say, in the crush of a crowded subway car. The idea of carrying around on one's person, waiting to be set off, one's own worst social nightmare was probably just too anxiety-inducing for most of us.

SUBPLANE

In the early 1960s, the U.S. Navy paid the Convair division of General Dynamics $36,000 to explore the feasibility of a flying submersible. The six-month study concluded that it was possible to build a jet-powered "subplane" that would be able to dive beneath the waves and cruise underwater. The two-man craft was designed to have an aircraft range of 300-500 nautical miles at speeds of 150 to 225 knots, together with an underwater range of 50 nautical miles at 5 knots and 75-foot depth. After landing like a conventional seaplane, the craft would seal off its jet engines and flood the hollow wings, tail, and sides of the hull, causing it to submerge. Underwater propulsion would be provided by battery-run propellors.

When the results of General Dynamic's research were made public, one man was not amused. He was Donald Reid, an inventor from Asbury Park, N.J., and he held U.S. Patent #3,092,060 for a flying submarine. If General Dynamics went forward with its program for the Navy, Mr. Reid intended to sue. As far as he was concerned, it was payback time.

Mr. Reid had been working on a flying submarine for over ten years. First he built a three-foot long, remote-controlled working model. In 1956 he took it to the Navy—from the Bureau of Naval Weapons to the Bureau of Ships, to the Office of Naval Research, to the Philadelphia Navy Yard, to the Submarine Base at New London.

"They sent me from one office to another just to give the fellows a good laugh," he recalled. "One man would say, 'Well, we think it's impossible but maybe so-and-so would be interested.' They called it the 'flub'; you know, flying sub."

Undeterred by the Navy's amusement, in 1957 Reid went straight to the top—President Eisenhower. Actually, he went to the White House where he was met at the gate by "a fellow who looked kind of Japanese" (his words), who listened to his story and took some notes. Though Eisenhower never contacted him directly, Reid read that when Ike took a ride aboard the *U.S.S. Seawolf*, he told the press that some day men would build flying submarines. Clearly, he'd gotten the message.

Reid next set about building a full-scale prototype in the apple orchard behind his house, using parts from wrecked airplanes scrounged from an airport dump. Cost-control was critical, as he had recently lost his job at an electronics factory and was living on unemployment insurance. Day and night he worked, a man possessed, spending his retirement funds once the unemployment checks ran out. The 28-foot-long torpedo-like craft had a 60-hp airplane engine mounted on top of a conning tower and an electrically-powered boat propeller on the stern. Neighbors were amused at the home-made contraption, but less so when Reid revved the engine and blew great blasts of dust through the closely-packed housing development.

The RFS (Reid Flying Submarine) was perfected in 1964. At a nearby river, Mr. Reid's son Bruce, the pilot, donned scuba gear for the dive test. (The conning tower was not watertight.) The RFS submerged and traveled at four knots about five feet beneath the surface. It then gurgled to the

surface. Bruce pumped out the wings, fuselage and pon-
toons, and removed a rubber bag from around the engine.
He took off and flew at 66 mph at an altitude of twenty feet
for four minutes—three minutes and 48 seconds longer
than the Wright brothers managed on their first flight.

In this, his moment of triumph, Reid read of the
Navy's contract with General Dynamics and felt betrayed.
As far as he was concerned, it was a clear case of high-
handed piracy. He immediately traveled to Washington,
D.C., and met with Eugene Handler, an engineer in the
Navy's Bureau of Weapons who was in charge of the

Navy's subplane program. Handler complimented Reid on his ingenuity and perseverance, but had to tell him the contract would remain with General Dynamics.

A bitter Donald Reid didn't know where to turn for justice. On his basement shortwave radio he tried reaching Senator Barry Goldwater, a fellow ham operator with an interest in unusual gadgetry. Unfortunately, the Senator was otherwise occupied, running for President against Lyndon Johnson. Though Reid felt protected by his patents, the Navy had its doubts. "Patents protect a particular design, not a general concept," Handler pointed out. "Reid has a patent on *his* flying submarine, but not on all conceivable designs for flying submarines."

The program never went anywhere, and so the issue never came to litigation. The anticipated problems proved too hard to overcome. Nearly all air-pockets in the plane would have to be able to be flooded and then pumped out, and this would include the air in partially-emptied fuel tanks. Engines had to be capable of being flooded, or else must occupy a small space when sealed against salt water. The engines had to be mounted high, for take-off from the water, and this posed aerodynamic problems. There were doubts about the kind of materials that would be practical, and how to ensure the survival of the crew.

Donald Reid received some recognition for his pioneering work on the flub. He was profiled in *The Saturday Evening Post*, gave lectures, and was paid $80 for appearing as a contestant on *I've Got a Secret*. He continued his work on bigger and better flying submarines, which would require more powerful engines. "I wish I could get my hands on a nuclear reactor," he told *The Saturday Evening Post*. "That sure would give me plenty of poop."

SUPERMARKET LIMBO

The New Products Showcase and Learning Center is a sort of limbo where supermarket products live on after death. Located in a large warehouse in Ithaca, New York, its shelves are crammed with some 80,000 products, including 5,500 different kinds of beverages and 3,600 shampoos. Of these, some 60,000 are no longer available; they are the has-beens, also-rans and never-weres of supermarket merchandise. The collection is the creation of Robert McMath, a former Colgate-Palmolive Co. executive who now makes his living writing and lecturing about product failure. McMath did not intentionally create a museum of failure. He buys a sample of every new supermarket item that hits the market, including those only test-marketed in limited areas; since 8 out of 10 new products fail, the law of averages is responsible for the poignant nature of his collection. It can be viewed by appointment only, and admission is not cheap. Food company executives pay thousands in consultation fees to try to learn the lessons of those who tried and flopped. A walking encyclopedia of marketplace rejects, McMath offers prognoses for new products based on the experience of the past. The next big trend he expected to flop? The "clear" fad in beverages.

The showcase has been called the National Hall of Shame and the Village of the Vanquished. A Nabisco executive, perhaps haunted by the sight of some of his own company's failures, called it the House of Lost Dreams. That's a sentiment that Mr. McMath shares; as he notes, no one brings out a product *expecting* it to fail.

Some of the disappointments on display:
- Hagar the Horrible Cola
- Panda Punch
- Sudden Soda ("The instant soda pop—just add water!")
- Pepsi A.M. (for those who need reassurance that it's all right to drink soda the first thing in the morning)
- Bird's Eye Soda Burst (instant ice cream soda)
- Devil Shake (a chocolate-flavored drink from Pepsi)
- Root Beer-Flavored Milk (from Dad's Root Beer)
- Yabba Dabba Dew
- Okeechobee Orange Pokem

- Quirst
- Kickapoo Joy Juice (from the moonshine Pappy Yokum drank in "L'il Abner")
- Nutrimato ("a delicious seasoned tomato-flavor cocktail with beef broth")
- Tuna Twist
- Koogle Peanut Spread (in chocolate, banana and cinnamon flavors)
- Tunies (Hot dogs made from tuna fish. Proved to be economically uncompetitive with hot dogs made from parts of cattle that no one would otherwise knowingly ingest.)
- Chocolate-covered pickled scallions
- Buffalo Chip chocolate cookies
- Jell-O for Salads (with flavors such as mixed vegetable, celery, and tomato)
- Legume Microwavable Sweet and Sour Tofu, Jofu luscious creamy tofu, Tofu Scrambler mix and To-Fitness Tofu Pasta. Tofu products in general have not done well.
- Burry "Happyniks" (chocolate and vanilla cookies with "happy faces" stamped into them)
- Shark Bites, a jerky-type snack made with real shark meat
- Muhammed Ali's Old Kentucky Cabin Barbecue Sauce ("It's the Greatest!")
- Frank Sinatra's spaghetti sauce
- Look of Buttermilk and Touch of Yogurt shampoos, and Gimmee Cucumber hair conditioner. None of these names apparently inspired confidence in those looking for that good hair day.
- Tri-Me, a laundry detergent concentrate that violated what must be an unwritten law of merchandising: Don't beg.
- Raggedy Ann and Andy his-and-her diapers
- Denim diapers (If only these had succeeded, Americans could go cradle to grave in blue jeans.)
- Male Chauvinist cologne
- Moonshine aftershave

THE SUSAN B. ANTHONY DOLLAR

On July 2, 1979 the U. S. Treasury introduced the Susan B. Anthony dollar, intended to take the place of the one dollar bill. Since the coin would last 15 years to the paper bill's eighteen months, it would save the government $50 million a year in printing costs. It had a raised, 11-sided border to make it easier for the visually-handicapped to identify. And it would be the first article of currency to carry the image of a woman other than Lady Liberty, thus honoring the contribution of women to American society. There was only one problem: the American people refused to accept it.

Plans to introduce the coin had begun four years earlier. The demand for dollar bills was increasing ten percent a year, and the Bureau of Printing and Engraving couldn't meet it without building a new $100 million facility. An outside consulting firm recommended that a new dollar coin be introduced: smaller than previous, bulky versions and able to fit in existing vending machines. Nevertheless, market research found that "There is a major potential for non-acceptance on the part of the general public, compounded by the fact that people have already gone through and rejected the $2 bill."

When the Carter administration decided to put the coin into production, Senator William Proxmire introduced a bill calling for the coin to honor Susan B. Anthony, a 19th-century suffragette. Women's groups from the National Organization of Women to the Daughters of the American Revolution expressed their support.

Frank Gasparro, chief designer for the mint, was given the job of designing the coin. He first depicted Susan B. Anthony as a young woman. Feminists complained that she had been too prettified. He tried to make her look older, adding a heavy brow, a hook to her nose, and a grim set to her jaw. Gasparro had his doubts, but the people at Treasury liked it fine.

The public didn't. Many described it as the ugliest thing they had ever seen. People didn't want to carry around pockets full of the heavy coins instead of dollar bills. And worst of all, it was too easily mistaken for a quarter. Every time you used it you found yourself saying, "Look, this is a dollar." Any motorist who inadvertently tossed a Susan B. Anthony into a toll basket instead of a quarter became a sworn enemy. For the same reason, merchants did not like handling it. People weren't ambivalent about the coin—they hated it. There were suspicions that some of the anger directed at the coin stemmed from hostility to feminism. Also, with the inflation of the late 1970s, a dollar that looked like a quarter was an unwelcome reminder of how far the mighty had fallen.

Director of the Mint Stella B. Hackel pointed out its advantages—it was shiny and clean, unlike a paper dollar which near the end of its short allotted span may resemble a used tissue. As to the coin's similarity to a quarter, Hackel argued that that should bother people no more than the one-dollar bill's similarity to a ten-dollar bill. Nevertheless, she was struck by the public's overwhelming prejudice against the "Suzy."

DWJ Associates, a public relations firm, was hired to try to improve the coin's image. "Our job was to get the good story out about the coin," said Michael Friedman, executive vice-president of the firm, who admitted that he himself had gotten tired of carrying the coins which nobody wanted. "We assumed there would be good stories to get out. There weren't."

By the spring of 1980, the mint had coined 840 million Susan B. Anthony dollars. 525 million sat in deep storage in federal vaults.

Ironically, the coin did enjoy an extended life in San Francisco porno parlors. Customers would enter a booth, drop their "Suzy" into a slot, and a curtain would rise to permit them a few minutes of conversation with a naked woman behind a glass partition.

TELEVISION, NOT READY FOR PRIME TIME

What defines a television show as a flop? It has to be more than being tacky, tawdry and utterly without merit, because we love shows like that. Even *My Mother the Car*, considered to be the worst show ever by most critics, lasted a full season. It should be fair to define as a flop any program that was never even considered for the regular schedule. Each year the networks hear about 4,000 story concepts, buy hundreds of scripts, and make about 90 pilots. Of these, perhaps twenty will become series. The following list is drawn from Lee Goldberg's *Unsold TV Pilots*. How they suffered by comparison to what's on is anyone's guess.

Dramas:

Clone Master. (NBC, 1978) A government scientist (Art Hindle) makes thirteen clones of himself and sends them out to fight crime. The adventures of one of the clones is the focus of each different episode.

Huggy Bear and the Turkey. (ABC, 1977) An intended spin-off of the Starsky and Hutch program, with jivey snitch Huggy Bear (Antonio Fargas) teaming up with strait-laced J. D. "Turkey" Turquet (Dale Robinette) to open a detective agency.

McClone. (NBC, 1988) Created by the same producer as *McCloud* (Glen Larson), it tells the story of a genetically-engineered soldier (Howie Long) who escapes from the secret military base where he was created, and roams America pursued by evil clones and government agents. Among other slip-ups in the sloppily-shot pilot, the city of Phoenix is made to stand in for New York, complete with palm trees in Central Park.

Microcops. (aka Micronauts; aka Meganauts) (CBS, 1989) The adventures of microscopic alien cops who come to Earth seeking an intergalactic criminal.

Samurai. (NBC, 1979) A Japanese-American district attorney in San Francisco by day, crime-fighting, sword-swinging samurai warrior by night.

Toni's Boys. (aka Toni's Devils) (ABC, 1980) An

attempt to spin-off the Charlie's Angels' format, with three buffed-up PI's (Bob Seagren, Stephen Shortridge, and Bruce Bauer) working for a mysterious matriarch (Barbara Stanwyck) and her butler (James E. Broadhead).

Weekend Nun. Crime drama. (ABC, 1972) Part-time nun, part-time probation officer. Starring Joanna Pettet.

Sitcoms:

Bungle Abbey. (NBC, 1981) The humorous hijinks of the wacky monks in Bungle Abbey. Directed by Lucille Ball.

Ethel is an Elephant. (CBS, 1980) A New York photographer shares his apartment with an abandoned baby circus elephant.

Which Way to the Mecca, Jack? (Independent, 1965) Fun and games with a swinging Middle Eastern sheik.

Pests. (NBC, 1982) A Nebraska man resettles in Manhattan, where he shares his apartment with a trio of three-foot tall, talking cockroaches.

Poochinski. (NBC, 1990) A tough-talking cop is killed in the line of duty and comes back as a talking, flatulent police dog determined to avenge his former incarnation.

Where's Everett? (CBS, 1966) The continuing adventures of a man (Alan Alda) who goes to pick up his morning paper and finds an abandoned invisible alien baby on his doorstep.

With the success of *Johnny Yuma* and *Johnny Ringo*, a number of pilots in the late fifties and early sixties put their faith in a title beginning with "Johnny." Some still do:

Johnny Bago. CBS, 1993. 1 Hour. Adventures of a small-time New York hood (Peter Dobson) on the lam in a Winnebago.

Johnny Dollar. CBS 1962. 30 minutes. Adventures of an insurance investigator (William Bryant).

Johnny Eager. MGM Television, 1959. A detective who owns a fleet of taxicabs.

Johnny Garage. CBS 4/13/83. 30 minutes. Troubles of a garage owner (Ron Carey).

Johnny Guitar. CBS 7/31/59. 30 minutes. Adventures of a singing cowboy (William Joyce).

Johnny Hawk. MCA 1958. A modern day sheriff (Floyd Simmons) uses both a car and a horse to fight crime.

Johnny Jupiter. DUM, 1953. A short-lived children's puppet show.

Johnny Mayflower. CBS 1958. Adventures of an orphan who comes to America on the Mayflower.

Johnny Moccasin. NBC 1956. A white boy (Jody McCrea) raised by Indians.

Johnny Risk. NBC 6/16/58. 30 minutes. Michael Landon as a gambler in the Yukon in the 1800s.

Johnny Wildlife. Screen Gems, 1958. Adventures of a wildlife photographer.

TESLA'S DEATH RAY, ETC.

There is a Charles Addams cartoon in which a patent attorney points a strange-looking device out his office window at the street below, while speaking disdainfully to the inventor beside him: "Death Ray—fiddlesticks! Why, it doesn't even slow them up!"

The chastened inventor could have easily been Nikola Tesla, who claimed to have invented a death ray that could destroy 10,000 airplanes at a distance of 250 miles. He also claimed to have received communication from other planets at his Colorado laboratory, to be able to photograph mental images on the retina of the eye, and to be capable, if he so desired, of splitting the Earth in two like an apple.

This is easy to laugh off if you are not aware that Tesla (1856-1943) was the towering genius who

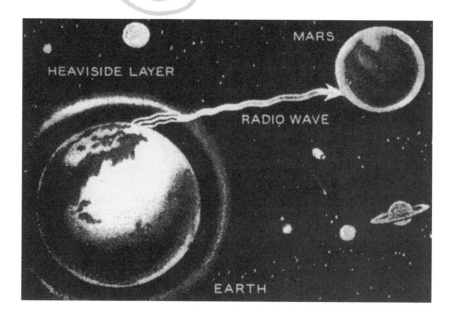

discovered the rotating magnetic field, the basis of all AC-powered machinery, and designed the first AC dynamos, transformers, and motors, as well as the power-generating operation at Niagra Falls. Among his 111 patents is one for the induction coil for radio and television—in fact, in a ruling in a patent dispute in 1943, the U. S. Supreme Court found that the principles behind Marconi's first radio broadcast in 1901 had all been described in detail by Tesla eight years earlier. He also invented fluorescent lighting, the arc-lamp, remote control and did preliminary work on the X-ray.

As a child in his native Serbia, Tesla displayed remarkable inventive talents. He said that when he visualized a new design, it was so real in his mind that he was able to test-run it and work out its bugs before committing it to paper. After emigrating to America he worked briefly for Thomas Edison, arguing the merits of alternating current over Edison's preferred direct current. AC won out as the industry standard. The Serbian immigrant's thinking was so advanced that many of his theories were derisively dismissed by his peers until he successfully demonstrated them. His remote-controlled model boat was shown before a crowd at Madison Square Garden in 1898. He also created lightning flashes 135 feet in length and claimed to have lighted 200 lamps at a distance of 25 miles without wires. This claim, which was never verified and has never been duplicated, was the basis of his prediction that the airplanes of the future would have electric motors which would be powered by energy beamed at them from the ground.

In 1900, backed by $150,000 from financier J. P. Morgan, Tesla began construction of a wireless World Broadcasting System tower on Long Island. It was intended to link all the world's telephone and telegraph services and transmit pictures, stock reports and weather warnings worldwide. Presumably, Tesla also intended to employ it for his wireless energy-transmission theory. The project was abandoned three years later when Morgan withdrew his support, leaving a 187-foot-tall wooden stucture topped with a wide copper dome, looking like an enormous mushroom. (Actually, it looked even more like an enormous something-else, as you might imagine.) This peculiar monument to Tesla's erratic genius stood until the First World War, when it was torn down for fear it would be used by German spies as an observation platform.

Tesla was fascinated by all forms of invisible energy, and in 1898 he conducted a number of experiments with the principle of natural resonance. Every object has its own natural frequency of vibration. An external source of vibrating force, tuned to its frequency, can start up sympathetic vibrations in the object—most of us have

ELECTRIC MOTORS RUN BY RADIO POWER

FUEL-LESS PLANE

RADIO POWER TRANSMITTER

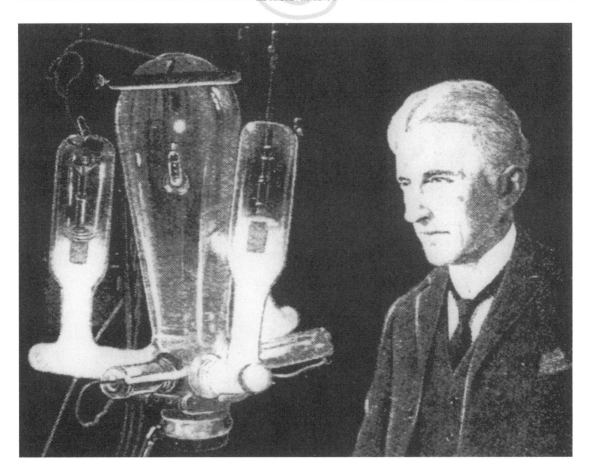

seen this demonstrated with a tuning fork in science class. If the object is of sufficient mass, these waves of energy can be quite powerful and potentially dangerous. Tesla connected a small oscillator (a vibration generator) to an iron pillar in his Manhattan laboratory. As the waves built up, a virtual earthquake was experienced in the surrounding city blocks, complete with trembling buildings, breaking windows and falling plaster. The police soon showed up at Tesla's lab to investigate the matter—as the neighborhood's resident mad scientist he was the obvious suspect. Tesla contended he could use the same principle to destroy the Empire State Building, Brooklyn Bridge, or with sufficiently large, properly placed and timed charges of dynamite, to split the Earth in half.

Tesla had many peculiar fixations: he had a fear of round objects, such as pearls or billiard balls, he counted things compulsively, calculated the volume of cups and bowls before eating from them, and obsessed about germs. He never married and allowed himself few friends (among them Mark Twain), and late in life his greatest joy was feeding pigeons and nursing sick ones in his apartment (apparently his germ-phobia made allowances for the flying rats). He had little business sense, and carelessly let many of the valuable technologies he pioneered go to the credit and enrichment of others. At the end of his life he was reduced to scribbling out his rush of ideas into notebooks, no longer having the resources to test them out. Scientists continue to study his notebooks for his insights.

3-D

In the early fifties, Hollywood was running scared. Movie ticket sales were falling, and hundreds of actors, writers and directors were fired by the studios. Americans were buying televisions and spending their evenings in their own living rooms rather than at theaters.

Hope to reverse this dismal trend came under the unlikely name of *Bwana Devil*, an independently-produced low-budget feature. Premiering on November 26, 1952, at two theaters in Los Angeles, it played to capacity crowds with lines stretching for blocks. One theater grossed $95,000 the first week. United Artists bought up the rights and made $15

million with its nationwide release. Its story was nothing special—a pair of man-eating lions attack railroad construction crews in Africa and have to be driven off with a hail of flying objects—but what drew the crowds was the new technology which made the lions seem to charge right off the screen and the projectiles fly into the audience. 3-D had arrived, and it appeared to be the wave of the future.

The 3-D process had existed for some time. In the Victorian period there was a craze for stereoscope viewers, in which two photos taken at slightly different angles seemed to blend into one three-dimensional image. Fifties-style 3-D used polarized glasses to join two filmed images shown by two separate projectors.

Of 3-D, a movie gossip columnist said, "Nothing since the atomic bomb has struck the motion picture industry with such force." The verdict was in—"flat" movies were passé. Hollywood scrambled to put "deepies" into production. The next 3-D pictures were released in the spring of 1953, *Man in the Dark* and *House of Wax*. *Man in the Dark* hurled scissors, spiders, knives, forceps, fists and falling bodies at its audience, as well as treated them to a roller coaster ride. "You've Never Been Scared Until You've Been Scared in 3-D!" read the promo for *House of Wax*, starring Vincent Price and Charles Bronson, probably the best 3-D film produced. For those who couldn't wait to see the movie, *Life* magazine printed some frames from it and included the 3-D glasses to view them. Both movies grossed over $15 million. The New York *Herald Tribune* said of 3-D that it "made every man a voyager to a brave new world." Studios rushed to meet the demand. By the end of the year, 100 million theater-goers had put on 3-D glasses, for which they paid an extra ten cent fee. The Polaroid Company, which made the requisite glasses, saw its stock price jump 33 percent.

Other deepies included *Fort Ti, Sangaree, Creature from the Black Lagoon, It Came from Outer Space, The French Line, Hondo, Kiss Me Kate, Miss Sadie Thompson, The Nebraskan* and *The Charge at Feather River*. But by the end of the year enthusiasm was wearing thin. A

THE DIRECTOR AND STARS OF *HOUSE OF WAX* APPEAR ASTONISHED BY THE 3-D PROCESS.

review of *Fort Ti* grumbled: "The lack of restraint is remarkable. To the injury of tomahawks, rifle shots, cannon balls, flaming arrows, broken bottles and blazing torches is added the insult of grubby redskins hurled judo style into one's lap." One peevish patron of *The Nebraskan* punched the theater owner afterward because he hadn't appreciated being boiled in oil.

The verdict was reversed. 3-D was an annoying fad whose time was spent. Viewers got tired of the gimmicks used to show off the effect, including even the thoroughly three-dimensional bust of Jane Russell. Many found that the process gave them headaches, especially if the two films were not perfectly synchronized. In Chicago the Board of Health closed 3-D theaters because the eyeglasses were full of germs. When *Kiss Me Kate* was released in both a 2-D and 3-D version, the "flattie" grossed 40% more. Hitchcock's *Dial M for Murder* was filmed in 3-D, but by the time it was completed the fad was dead and only the conventional print was released. The idea that 3-D would save Hollywood was as illusory as the effect itself. 1953 turned out to be even worse than the slump year of 1952, with money invested in 3-D technology down the drain. The new panacea? CinemaScope, Cinerama, Vista Vision, Superama, Glamarama and Todd-A-O—the wide screen.

3-D continues to pop up as a novelty in movies such as Warhol's *Frankenstein*, *Friday the 13th Part III*, *Jaws 3-D*, *Spacehunter*, and *Amityville 3-D*. The soft-core porno film *The Stewardesses* (1969), in which something besides arrows and fists was shoved in the viewer's face, is reputed to be the highest grossing 3-D movie to date.

TOILET SEATS

Most of us would regard the toilet seat as a design problem that has been satisfactorily resolved, like the crowbar or the paper clip. Nevertheless, there's no stopping progress, and the following are some improvements on the toilet seat that have been patented, though none has yet achieved widespread use.

- Toilet Lid Lock, (U.S. Patent #3,477,070), prevents unauthorized access to the toilet bowl. Considering the alternatives, is this really a good idea?

- Whisper Seat, (U.S. Patent #3,593,345), is a toilet seat with an acoustical barrier that prevents embarrassing sounds from being heard by other people.

- Toilet Seat Clock Apparatus, (U.S. Patent #5,182,823), is a toilet seat with a small digital clock set into the front. It's intended to help the morning user to keep track of how much time remains before departure for work or school. The clock may put in so as to be readable for someone sitting on the seat, or reversed for someone standing in front of it. Even when the lid is down, a slot in the cover makes the clock visible.

- Toilet Seat Cover Position Alarm, (U.S. Patent #4,849,742), is a fairly complex device involving an electric switch set under the toilet seat and a float switch in the tank. It sets off an alarm if the toilet seat is left up for too long after the toilet is flushed.

- Super Bowll 2000 was on display at the 1987 Fad Fair III at New York's Sheraton Centre Hotel. It was a luminescent toilet seat invented by two twin sisters from California, Joyce and Jackie Giunta.

"She and I dream a lot of the same dreams," said Joyce. "I was the first one to mention the idea of a toilet seat that glows in the dark, but as soon as I said it my sister said, 'God, you know, I just thought of the *same thing.*' So we both saw a need and we're ready to fulfill that need."

The sisters projected that their seat would be a fixture "in every house in America by the year 2000."

TOPLESS SWIMSUIT

The late 1950s and early 1960s were a high watermark in America's Cult of the Breast. Jayne Mansfield was a star. Barbie was introduced. Russ Meyers made movies. Playboy magazine was on the cutting edge of societal evolution. Into this fevered atmosphere stepped designer Rudy Gernreich with his topless bathing suit in 1964. It was black, and ended above the navel like the midriff-controlling panty girdles still common at the time. A pair of

THIS MODEST MODEL WEARS A TOPLESS SWIMSUIT KNOCK-OFF.

stringy suspenders rose from the center, between the bared breasts and over the shoulders. Reaction was immediate, intense, and international. The Vatican newspaper, *L'Osservatore Romano*, devoted an article to the topless bathing suit headlined "The Ultimate Shame." The Pope condemned it as a "desperate and senseless adventure of impudent shamelessness." *Isvestia*, the Soviet newspaper, weighed in under the headline, "Back to Barbarism." The topless suit was a symptom of capitalist sickness: "So the decay of the money-bags society continues," it declared. A Baptist minister brought pickets to march in front of a Dallas department store that displayed the suit in its windows. "We Protest These Suits in the Name of Christ," read their placards. The Republican Party used the suit as a symbol of decadence in the 1964 campaign.

Comedians weighed in. "The police are apprehensive of what these suits will reveal," said Mort Sahl. "I'm apprehensive they'll reveal nothing." And from Phyllis Diller, "When I wore one, everyone thought I was Albert Schweitzer." Art Buchwald wrote that "1964 was the year the bottom fell out of the top."

The topless swimsuit was one of the major stories of 1964. News magazines usually showed the topless bathing suit from the back, or with the model demurely covering herself. *Life* magazine permitted one fully-exposed underwater shot under the "news-nudes" policy, by which the demands of journalistic integrity are occasionally permitted to override strictures against nudity for purely prurient reasons. *The New York Times* called it "the most radical development in swimsuit design since the bikini."

Where had it come from? It sprang from an off-hand remark. In an interview, Gernreich, the California designer who had pioneered many of the swimsuit trends of the fifties and sixties, was asked where he thought the future lay. "In five years every American woman will be wearing a bathing suit that is bare above the waist," answered Gernreich, thinking of what he had observed in the south of France. Then it occurred to him that if the topless suit was really coming, his status as a designer demanded that he be the one to design it.

The idea proved an unexpected challenge. "I really did think that people with beautiful bodies would drop their bikini tops," Gernreich said at the time. "But just a bikini bottom would be the *end* of design." Early sketches looked like trunks or, worse yet, boxer shorts. He added straps to the boxer shorts "for pure décor."

There were no plans to manufacture the design; it was a prediction, not a product. But along with the publicity, orders came in. There was no choice but to

TOPLESS SWIMSUIT

fill them. Why would anyone buy it? Shana Alexander, writing in *Life*, offered two possibilities. "One is the fashion feedback effect—fashion-conscious women buy it because Rudi Gernreich designed it. The other reason is strictly feminine. If a woman is going to appear naked, she somehow prefers to appear naked in something designed for the purpose, not in half of last year's bikini."

John Frederic designed a spectacularly dumb wide-brimmed hat with flaps that let down to cover those parts that Gernreich exposed. Jumping on the bandwagon, a San Diego manufacturer put out a "convertible topless swimsuit" with a removable top. Carnegie Models, Ltd., a British clothier, came out with a topless cocktail dress. Mary Quant, who gave us the miniskirt, announced plans for two topless dresses. The acceptance of toplessness in previous periods—Minoan Crete, Classical Egypt, 18th Century Europe—suggested that the time was right for a revival. Alas, it was not to be.

Only three thousand topless bathing suits were ever sold (at $24), and few were ever worn in public. In addition to being illegal it was no good for swimming and Shana Alexander noted the "disastrous strap marks" it would leave on the sunbather. Gernreich got all he could have wanted out of it—further notoriety as a fashion rogue. But as a predicter and promoter of this trend, he was strictly a flop.

TREPANNING

In the 1960s England once again exerted her imperial power over America, this time in matters trendy. Music, fashion and films from the mother country were exported to the former colonies, where they were ecstatically embraced. One novel concept of the English counterculture failed to elicit much enthusiasm here, or anywhere else for that matter: trepanning.

Trepanning, or making a small hole through the skull, is one of the oldest operations performed by man. Skulls of Neanderthals have been found that were successfully trepanned, as well as those of members of the noble and priestly castes in the more advanced ancient cultures. Until the 20th Century, madness was often treated with trepanation, the hole in the skull being seen as a way to release inner demons or later, to relieve pressure on the brain. In 1962 it was advanced as a path to higher consciousness by a Dutch self-styled guru, Bart Huges. It was his theory that the state of one's consciousness is determined by the quantity of blood in the brain. When man began to walk upright, he argued, gravity tended to draw the blood to his lower regions, thus limiting his ability to reach a higher consciousness. One could address the problem by standing on one's head, taking drugs (which he believed increased the brain's blood supply), or by jumping from hot baths into cold water. All of these solutions were merely temporary, however. Huges noted that from birth through early childhood the skull is not completely closed, and thus the pulsation of blood around the brain is not inhibited by the enclosed carapace. He associated this fact with the enormous learning that takes place during this period and the dreams, imagination and intense perception of the child. The best way to return to this state, he reasoned, was by drilling a small hole through the head. He did so to himself. Feeling immediate beneficial results, he began proselytizing the process, which earned him a spell in a Dutch lunatic asylum.

Shortly after his release he met an Englishman, Joseph Mellen, who was to become his greatest (actually, only) disciple. Huges sheparded Mellen through his first LSD trip, and the two were much in demand in 1966 for lectures and interviews on the ballyhooed drug. One interview was given to two reporters from London's Sunday newspaper *The People*. The reporters seemed fascinated by what Huges had to say about LSD, the theory of "Brainbloodvolume," and trepanning. To such a receptive audience, Huges went on at considerable length. To his disappointment, the story that appeared was headlined: "THIS DANGEROUS IDIOT SHOULD BE THROWN

OUT." Nevertheless, Huges and Mellen had many friends in the London avant-garde, and their ideas found some sympathetic ears. The playwright Heathcote Williams made a trepanation scene the climax of his award-winning play, *AC-DC*. Julie Felix, an American folk-singer popular in London, promoted the doctrine of trepanation in some of her songs, such as *Brainbloodvolume* and *The Great Brain Robbery*.

The time came when Joey Mellen felt it was time to practice what he had preached. Unable to find a doctor willing to perform the operation, he poked around in medical supply stores until he found a trepanning instrument, a kind of auger designed to be worked by hand. It had a spike at the cener of a cylindrical saw. Driven into the skull, the spike would hold the apparatus in place while the revolving saw cut out a disc of bone. This was cheaper than an electric drill, and Mellen felt it would allow him to more carefully manage the delicate procedure. However, it was more difficult than he had expected, akin to trying to uncork a bottle of wine from the inside. (The fact that he anesthetized himself for the operation with a dose of LSD may have hampered his efforts.) After the botched attempt, he contacted Huges, now back in Holland. Unfortunately, having been officially designated an undesirable alien, Huges could not come to his assistance. Mellen made several further attempts and finally the operation succeeded. In his published account of the experience, *Bore Hole*, Mellen describes the sensation: "there was an ominous-sounding schlurp and the sound of bubbling. I drew the trepan out and the bubbling continued. It sounded like air bubbles running under the skull as they were pressed out. I looked at the trepan and there was a bit of bone in it. At last!" Though reassured by the schlurping noise, the irregularity of the disc of bone he had removed left him doubting that he had made a proper hole. A few months later he repeated the operation with an electric drill applied just above his hairline, drilling an inch into his head. The result was all he had hoped for. He felt his spirits rising higher and higher until he reached a state of serenity he claims has been with him ever since. His girlfriend, Amanda Fielding, followed suit. Her self-administered operation was captured on a home movie they titled *A Heartbeat in the Brain*. They have shown it on their lecture tours in England and America. Amanda Fielding has run twice for Parliament on a platform demanding that trepanning be available from the National Health Service. The second time she received 139 votes.

In thrall to fashion, people have pierced their ears, nostrils, lips, tongues and nipples. Safety pins through the cheek enjoyed a brief vogue. In the quest for a higher consciousness, though, few have been willing to follow the cranium-perforating example of Huges and Mellen.

TURN-ON

In January of 1968, *Rowan and Martin's Laugh-In* debuted on NBC. A fast-paced hour of one-liners, sight-gags, blackouts and short skits, *Laugh-In* brought topical humor and a hip attitude to television. The show was an immediate hit, made stars of several of its performers and contributed a slew of catch-phrases to the vernacular, such as "Here come de judge," "You bet your bippy," "Sock it to me," and "The Fickle Finger of Fate Award."

On the heels of their success, *Laugh-In* producers George Schlatter and Ed Friendly, and Digby Wolfe, one of its production executives, were asked by the advertising boss of Bristol-Meyers to develop a new half-hour series, "something unusual and provocative." As it happened, they had a concept that they had been kicking around prior to *Laugh-In*. Described as "a satire on our dehumanized society," *Turn-On*, according to Digby Wolfe, was to be a "visual, comedic, sensory assault involving...animation, videotape, stop-action film, electronic distortion, computer graphics—even people." Schlatter described its innovative techniques: "It was the first time the Moog synthesizer was used. We also used shadowless light, multiple images, dioptic lenses, and a laugh track that was programmed into a computer. The host was a computer."

Both NBC and CBS were shown the pilot and rejected it. "It wasn't any good," said an NBC programmer. "It wasn't funny, and in many areas it was in bad taste." CBS concurred, a spokesman saying, "We said 'no, thank you.' Not so much because the show was dirty but because there wasn't a joke in it. Also it was so fast with the cuts and chops that some of our people actually got physically disturbed by it."

A second pilot was filmed, somewhat less tawdry and frenetic, and ABC expressed interest. The two pilots were shown at its affiliates meeting and the response was positive. In one of those instances of mass delusion that often attends the introduction of a flop, everyone agreed that the Schlatter-Friendly lightning had struck again and that the show was destined for a spot in the top ten.

Turn-On was broadcast on Wednesday, February 5, 1969, and never, ever again. Despite the high expectations and technical innovations, *Turn-On's* chief distinction was the unrelenting vulgarity of its skits. One revolved around a vending machine that dispensed birth control pills. An animated airplane towed a banner across the screen with gags about homosexuality such as: "God Save the Queens," "The Amsterdam Levee Is a Dike," and "Free Oscar Wilde." The longest skit, lasting several minutes, seemed to make the biggest impression. It featured the word "SEX" repeatedly flashing on the screen, in large letters with different colors and emphasis—"SEX!", "SEX?", etc.—as guest host Tim Conway and Bonnie Boland flitted in and out of the frame, mugging suggestively at each other. The show that was supposed to have been daring and different came off as the dirty, distilled dregs of *Laugh-In*.

Before the program was over, stations were flooded with negative calls. The Denver affiliate canceled it halfway through, with an announcement that "The remainder of this show won't be seen." The general manager of WEWS in Cleveland wired the president of ABC: "If your naughty little boys have to write dirty words on the walls, please don't use *our* walls." Two days later, 75 stations, nearly half of those carrying the program, had dropped it. Within the week ABC cancelled it.

Turn-On had earned its place in history as one of television's greatest flops. Don't expect to see it on some future retrospective, either; as part of the settlement with the networks and sponsors, it was agreed that the tapes would be locked up and never shown again.

The *Turn-On* debacle taught ABC a lesson, and as a result the network turned down another controversial comedy concept that was offered to them a few months later. It dealt with risque material and disparaged African-Americans and Jews, so why take a chance? *All In the Family* went to CBS.

UNDERPANTS

Some recent high points in underpants:

Snif-T-Panties were put on the market by a Miami company in 1975. The scented women's underwear came in a variety of fragrances, including rose, banana, popcorn, pickle—and for the stimulation of real men—whiskey, and pizza.

Israeli scientists invented electronic underpants for the incontinent in 1978. Moisture-sensitive electrodes in the cloth sounded a buzzer when activated by urine. And you thought it was distracting hearing people's *beepers* go off at the movies.

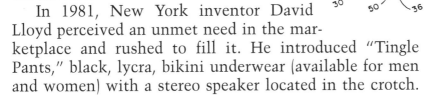

In 1981, New York inventor David Lloyd perceived an unmet need in the marketplace and rushed to fill it. He introduced "Tingle Pants," black, lycra, bikini underwear (available for men and women) with a stereo speaker located in the crotch.

They were equipped with a jack that enabled them to be hooked up to the output mode of a stereo.

Frederick's of Hollywood, makers of licentious lingerie, produced a pair of panties with a battery-powered sound chip. Mood music available for a romantic evening includes "Jingle Bells," "Love Me Tender," "Let Me Call You Sweetheart," "Happy Birthday," "Here Comes the Bride," and "When the Saints Go Marching In."

The Honda Motor Company's bi-annual inventiveness contest for employees has unearthed some unique innovations, but none to match 6-Day Underwear, the 1987 winner. According to the story in the *Wall Street Journal*, the underwear has three leg holes, which enables it to last for six days without washing. The wearer rotates it 120 degrees on each of the first three days, and then turns it inside out and repeats the process. (Using the same process, an ordinary two-legged pair of underwear should be good for four days.)

They used to say that doing it with a condom on was like eating a candy bar without removing the wrapper, but such are the times. For those who require the maximum protection, a patent was granted in 1990 for a jock-strap that securely mounts a condom in front. Secured between two mounting plates, the condom cannot slip off in use. The surrounding material offers a further barrier to contact with the sex partner. If you're still nervous, try scuba gear.

UP OR DOWN BY BELT

A remarkably unsafe-looking mode of tranportation was featured in a 1930s issue of *Modern Mechanix*. Billed as useful to mills, factories, offices and other places where there is constant run of employees from one floor to another, it was a sort of vertical escalator. Openings about three feet square were arrayed one above another through the floors of a building. Through them traveled an endless conveyor belt with tiny platforms attached at regular intervals. About four feet above each platform was a horizontal handrail. The belt fit into a slotted frame at either

UP or DOWN by BELT

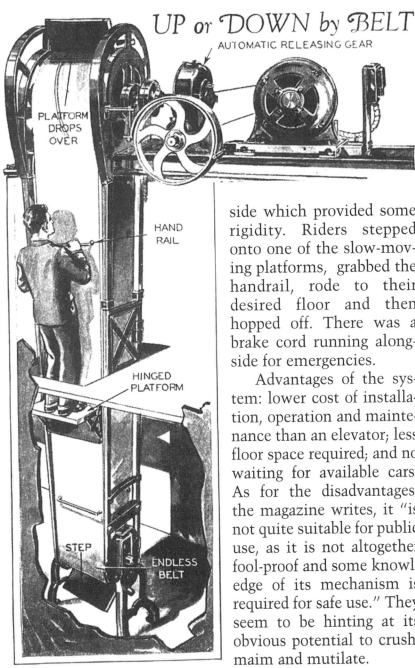

AUTOMATIC RELEASING GEAR

PLATFORM DROPS OVER

HAND RAIL

HINGED PLATFORM

STEP

ENDLESS BELT

side which provided some rigidity. Riders stepped onto one of the slow-moving platforms, grabbed the handrail, rode to their desired floor and then hopped off. There was a brake cord running alongside for emergencies.

Advantages of the system: lower cost of installation, operation and maintenance than an elevator; less floor space required; and no waiting for available cars. As for the disadvantages, the magazine writes, it "is not quite suitable for public use, as it is not altogether fool-proof and some knowledge of its mechanism is required for safe use." They seem to be hinting at its obvious potential to crush, maim and mutilate.

The conveyances were actually used in Great Britain, where a few reportedly exist to this day. They have been dubbed the "Pater Noster" (Our Father) because their passengers tend to be moved to prayer.

VENDING MACHINE VENGEANCE

Vending machines have been around since 219 B.C., when Hero Cstebus of Alexandria installed a coin-operated holy water dispenser in a Greek temple. Worshippers dropped a five-drachma coin through a slot, and the weight of it briefly opened a valve and dispensed the holy water. There was no built-in precaution against the use of slugs—security was left to the wrath of the gods. Not until the end of the nineteenth century did we begin to see vending machines as we know them today, selling postcards, railroad tickets, chocolate, gum, and cigarettes. The French had wine vendors as well as the "Parfumez-Vous," which delivered a spray of perfume.

"Convenience" has been one of the great driving forces in American marketing, and the coin-operated vendors seemed to provide it. Some of the many innovations reached a bit too far, though, and were not long with us.

- In 1961, the Grand Union supermarket chain lined entire storefronts with machines selling grocery items. The 24-hour service offered at the "Food-O-Matic" never paid off. When the stores were open, customers bought inside, and at night there wasn't enough traffic to justify the complications of stocking and servicing the machines.
- "Dial-A-Sale" was the world's largest vending machine, at five-feet wide, five-feet deep and nine-feet high. It stocked up to 204 different items on shelves mounted on a conveyor belt. After depositing the proper change, the customer punched in the desired code number and the belt turned until the appropriate shelf was behind one of the sliding doors. It was intended to be installed as a mini-department store in residential areas and apartment buildings.
- In 1961, Pat Boone planned to open 96 Dine-O-Mats. They would have featured food dispensed by vending machines which would then have been heated by self-service microwave ovens.
- When Macy's installed a men's underwear vending machine in June, 1960, it made national news. So

many people crowded in to get a look at the contraption that management moved it from the ground level to the fifth floor to prevent traffic tie-ups near the entrance. Despite customer curiosity, sales did not justify the innovation's continuation.

- In 1970 Billy N. Utz, aide to West Virginia Senator Harry Byrd, Jr., received a patent on a liquor-vending machine that passed judgment on its customers. The buyer had to prove he was of drinking age by inserting an identification card into the machine. He then took a sobriety test based on how fast his eyes could follow a moving object. If the buyer did not meet the requirements, no liquor was dispensed.

- "What's the latest dope on Wall Street? My son-in-law." As if there weren't already enough reasons to kick vending machines, in 1971 two Dallas firms developed one which, for a dime, delivered a

Henny Youngman joke along with a candy bar. Ussery Industries was to blame for the idea and Test Equipment Corp. took responsibility for making it technically feasible. Youngman taped 230 of his best-worn gags for the project, such as "Hey! My mother-in-law tried a mudpack treatment on her face, and for two days she looked great. Then the mud fell off." Ussery expected to place 5,000 of the vaudevenders in service.

- Later in the same year Castagna Electronics of Brooklyn, N.Y., came up with an attachment for cigarette machines that delivered a 20-second commercial as soon as a coin was dropped in. With cigarette commercials recently banned from radio and television, it was expected to be embraced by competing tobacco companies eager to pitch the customer at the point of purchase. The ACMRU (Audio Commercial Message Repeating Unit) could deliver 16 to 20 different spoken messages or singing jingles. It was intended for use in high traffic areas, where the commercials could be heard by anyone within twenty feet. Wouldn't people find this annoying? The promoter graciously observed that "you don't have to stand there and listen to it."

WEENIE WHIRL, ETC.

In his 1991 autobiography, *Life Is Too Short*, Mickey Rooney describes some of the less successful ventures he has backed over the years. One was the Weenie Whirl restaurant chain he launched in 1980, named after the O-shaped hot dogs he planned to serve. They fit on hamburger buns, and the hole in the middle could accomodate a variety of garnishes, each suggesting a name for the sandwich. His menu included the Yankee Doodle (cheese), the Micklish (relish), the Eric von Weenie (sauerkraut), the Pancho Weenie (chili), and the Surfboard Weenie (raisins and pineapple). Other fast food franchises that occurred to him were Mickey Rooney's Star-B-Que, Rooney Shortribs, and Mickey Rooney Macaroni.

Rooney also came up with an aerosol product that sprayed something onto your scalp that was supposed to look like hair, but looked more like cotton candy. It stuck there until you washed it off, or got rained on. It was called Complete, for the Man Who Wants to Be. Ron Popeil of Ronco fame recently made a fortune pitching the same sort of thing on late-night TV, but not Mickey.

Then there was a new concept in underwear Rooney proposed to Fruit of the Loom: disposable underpants for men and women who traveled and couldn't be bothered with dirty laundry. They would be called "Rip Offs." To complete the women's set, there would also be bras, called "Tip Offs." Fruit of the Loom gave him the Brush Off, which he attributed to the well-known "not invented here" syndrome.

Rooney approached Ralston Purina with a perfectly sensible thought. "You make great dog and cat food," he told them, "but you don't market anything for our pets to drink. You could make a lot of money with doggie drink, puppy pop, and kitty cola." The drinks would be sugar-free concoctions full of healthy vitamins and minerals. No sale.

He set up a pharmaceutical company and named it Elim. That enabled him to give his products snappy names: Elim-N-Ache, for headaches; Elim-N-Ate, a laxative; Elim-A-Weight, for dieters; Elim-N-Itch, a foot powder. Showing a similar talent for slogans was Trapeze, the perfume line he tried to launch: "There's Danger in Every Drop." And the drink he came up with called Thirst, with the slogan: "Thirst Come, Thirst Served."

WIN BUTTONS

With inflation running at 12 percent when he took office in 1974, Gerald Ford felt that strong measures were needed. He convened a "summit" conference on inflation, and soon afterwards addressed the nation. Ford pointed to a large button on his lapel that said WIN, and asked every American to help him "Whip Inflation Now." Americans who wrote to the White House would receive a WIN button of their own to show that they had enlisted in the fight. As more and more Americans pinned on WIN buttons, inflation would presumably be frightened into retreat. The program was greeted by a chorus of hoots and guffaws, and died quietly shortly thereafter.

Being a middle-aged Republican, President Ford was not too hip to pop culture. He hadn't gotten the word that buttons had been passé for about five years; by the mid-1970s, T-shirts were the preferred mode of self-expression.

WINE AND DINE DINNER

Heublin, Inc., known as a purveyor of alcoholic beverages, brought out Wine and Dine dinners. Entrees such as chicken chablis and beef chianti came packaged with one of those airline-sized bottles of wine. Customers who did not bother to read the directions assumed that the wine was intended to be enjoyed with their meal, but if so their enjoyment was short-lived. The bottle contained a cheap, salty, cooking wine, intended to be stirred into the entree during preparation. Despite the message *"Not for Beverage Use"* in fancy script on its label, confusion over this procedure caused customers to wine and dine elsewhere.

WOMEN'S URINALS

According to Frank Muir's *An Irreverent and Almost Complete History of the Bathroom*, until the early nineteenth century, ladies were accustomed to relieving themselves discreetly almost anywhere when in public. "They wore long dresses and no drawers, so it was simply a matter of standing astride some sort of gutter and gazing dreamily about for a minute or so." As in so many other ways, progress has made things more complicated. Esquire's "Dubious Achievement Awards" for 1991 included a news item that Baltimore Orioles officials were considering installing the "She-inal," a device that enables women to urinate standing up, in the women's rooms of their new stadium.

The She-inal was the creation of Urinette, Inc., a Pensacola, Florida company that believes it has broken one of the final barriers to equality of the sexes. Though their deal with the Baltimore Orioles fell through, they continue to market the (according to them) first effective urinal designed by and for women. Haven't seen it around? "Our product is the microwave of the bathroom," says Urinette inventor Kathie Jones, recalling the lengthy resistance to that particular innovation.

Why a urinal for women? Urinette's surveys reveal that 90 percent of women never sit directly on the seat in a public restroom, either hovering above it or covering the seat with toilet paper. 7 percent actually admitted that they stand in a squatting position on the toilet seat itself. Urine being sterile, a repository exclusively for urine is inherently more sanitary than the usual toilet. In addition, a urinal uses less water for flushing and requires less floor space.

Though it may be the great untold story of the toilet fixtures industry,

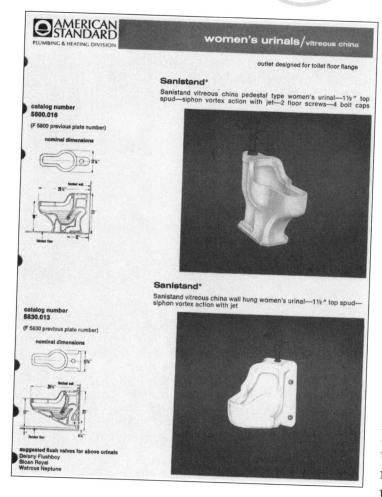

AMERICAN STANDARD
PLUMBING & HEATING DIVISION

women's urinals/vitreous china

outlet designed for toilet floor flange

Sanistand
Sanistand vitreous china pedestal type women's urinal—1½" top spud—siphon vortex action with jet—2 floor screws—4 bolt caps

catalog number
5800.016
(F 5800 previous plate number)
nominal dimensions

Sanistand
Sanistand vitreous china wall hung women's urinal—1½" top spud—siphon vortex action with jet

catalog number
5830.013
(F 5630 previous plate number)
nominal dimensions

suggested flush valves for above urinals
Delany Flushboy
Sloan Royal
Watrous Neptune

women's urinals have been available since the late 1930s. Kohler offered the "Hygia," American Standard the "Sanistand," and Crane the "Hy-San." Unfortunately, all of these fixtures were designed by men, and women find them almost impossible to use. They required that a woman remove her underwear or hobble with it stretched between her ankles, hold up her skirt and straddle a trough extending out from the wall. Because of the level of undressing necessary, they were usually installed in a privacy booth. On the wall above them there was usually a sign explaining their use, as well as an explicit reminder that they were for urine only. (Their similarity to a toilet posed the danger that some might use it as such.) Industry spokesmen claim that the demise of women's urinals was due to, in a word, pantyhose, but it is hard to imagine they could have been convenient at the best of times. With pants they seem almost impossible. Considering their inconvenience and the potential for mishaps, there seems to be little to recommend the entire notion. The companies still have warehouses full of them, if anyone's interested.

When the military refurbished barracks to accommodate female soldiers, men's urinals were sometimes replaced with the problematic female design. Considering that the women in the Army dress exclusively in pants, blame for this decision undoubtedly belongs with some male procurement officer. One female soldier reported that after looking over the women's urinals in her barracks, troops could come up with only one practical use for them. They filled them with soil, planted flowers in them, and saw to it that they were watered with one flush daily.

A different solution to the same problem was marketed by the Aplex Company of San Mateo, California. Called Le Funelle, it was a collapsible paper funnel similar to those triangular cups that go with a water cooler. With this device pressed against her, a woman could pee standing up. It was widely advertised in San Francisco, but even in that fabled city the demand was not sufficient.

X-RAY SHOE FITTING

A common sales promotion device at shoe stores in the late 1940s and early 1950s, the shoe-fitting X-Ray unit promised to match customers to their ideal footwear. Customers tried on a pair of shoes, then put their feet into a pair of holes at the bottom of the machine to view the fit on a fluoroscopic screen at the top. There were three viewing ports at the top—one for the salesman, one for the shoe buyer, and one for parents if the shoes were for a child. The now-defunct Adrian X-Ray Co. of Milwaukee manufactured some 10,000 of them.

The problem: rampant radiation leakage. Though the box was lead-lined, there was no seal around the footholes or viewing ports. Avid comic book readers may find it hard to understand why all that radioactive energy bathing their bodies didn't produce legions of super-powered shoe sales-

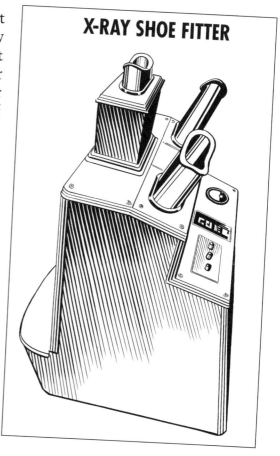

X-RAY SHOE FITTER

man. By 1970 the machines were banned in all states, though some shoe stores used them as recently as the 1980s.

YUGO, AND ITS ANTECEDENTS

The auto manufacturing tradition behind the Iron Curtain is not a proud one. There was the Czechoslovakian Skoda, and the Russian Lada, described as "looking like a Fiat put together in dim light." The East Germans had the mellifluously-named Wartburg and the abominable Trabant, often described as the worst car that has ever been built. "Trabant" means satellite, and it was designed in 1958 as a tribute to Sputnik, communism's great claim to technological superiority. Though it may have honored Sputnik, it certainly did not honor technological superiority, as in thirty-two years of continuous production it did not incorporate one stylistic or mechanical improvement. Spewing a smoke screen of exhaust in its wake, the Trabant emitted nine times more hydrocarbons and five times more carbon monoxide than the average Western car. Its body was made of a primitive sort of plastic that released toxic fumes when burned. Before unification, the "Trabi" had a lock on the market in East Germany and sold some three million, though its shortcomings inspired mordant jokes. One suggested that if it had two tailpipes it would make a fine wheelbarrow. Another told of a wealthy Texan who heard about the three year waiting list to purchase a Trabant. Figuring it must be a heck of a car if people were willing to wait so long for one, he sent off a sizable check. Delighted with the hard currency, the factory director shipped him one right away. "Those Germans are really something," said the Texan, impressed. "While I'm waiting for my Trabant they sent me this full-size plastic model!" Since reunification, the wholesale abandonment of unwanted Trabants on German streets has been a major problem. According to *Fortune*, the West Germans considered investing in a bioengineered microbe that would eat the plastic junkers, but worried that such a creation might get out of control with unforeseen results. *Revenge of the Trabi Eaters*?

In 1985, when the Yugoslavian car maker Zavodi Crvena Zastava (Red Flag Enterprises) broke into the U.S. market, it had to overcome this unfortunate legacy. First, it stressed that Yugoslavia was, in fact, *not* an East-bloc nation. Secondly, it entered the One Lap of America rally, coming in a respectable third. Thirdly, it priced the Yugo GV at $3900, making it the cheapest car on the market.

When it first arrived in showrooms, the Yugo aroused considerable interest. The name was a cute play on words, though Jay Leno claimed it sounded like Boris Karloff's cousin from New Jersey. The price was definitely right. Unfortunately, the Yugo's slogan might as well have been "You Get What You Pay For." Of all inexpensive compacts tested by *Changing Times* in 1988, it had the worst handling, braking, and acceleration (0-60 in 17.6 seconds). In a five-mile-an-hour crash test it managed to sustain $2,756 worth of damage—more than two-thirds its value. It rated lowest overall by a considerable margin. In its small car round-up, *Playboy* classified it under "Lawn Tractors for the Masses." Yugo America went through management changes, and for 1989 promised the most generous auto warranty ever—for the first year, all parts and maintenance, including routine oil changes, would be free. That sort of offer raises suspicions of the "methinks thou doth protest too much" variety. Yugo America spoke of a coming sleek four-door model, that Senior Vice President Tony Ciminera claimed would be snazzy and dependable. "You won't even know it's a Yugo," he added, tactlessly.

The Yugo peaked in 1987, with 48,800 sales—not bad, but far lower than expectations. Plagued by defects and poor dealer support, the Yugo earned an inevitable nickname: "The Edsel of the Eighties." After a bankruptcy reorganization in 1989, only 3,100 Yugos were sold in the United States in 1991. In 1992 its factory ceased production, a victim, finally, of Yugoslavia's civil war.

ZEPPELIN, RETURN OF THE

"Zeppelin's New Age of Air Travel" is the cover story of the July, 1994, issue *Popular Mechanics*. An artist's conception shows the latest proposal for a passenger dirigible over the Manhattan skyline. Inside, we read that the Luftschiffbau Zeppelin, the great Geman airship firm, proposes to build the LZ N30, a dirigible that could carry between fifty and eighty paying passengers. The rigid frame (a dirigible is rigid, as opposed to a blimp, which holds its shape by gas pressure) would be constructed from space-age materials and would incorporate features such as vectoring propellor units that would improve the airship's handling. Its lift would be provided by 1 million cubic feet of helium, rather than the explosive hydrogen that gave the Zeppelin company such a public relations black-eye in 1937.

The project sounds intriguing, but don't book passage just yet. In 1991 *Popular Mechanics* headlined a story, "Rebirth of the Blimp." And in 1983, it was "Airships Rise Again." And in 1971, "Don't Sell the Airship Short." And in 1958, "Who Said the Blimp is All Through?" This is not to pick on *Popular Mechanics*. A perusal of the *Reader's Guide to Periodical Literature* over the past forty years shows such articles popping up almost annually. Like Big Bands, Zeppelin passenger travel is one of those things that keeps coming back but somehow never gets here.

In the thirties, the great airships were the trendy way for the wealthy to cross the Atlantic, like the Concorde is today. The 2 1/2 to 3-day passage offered a level of luxury and spaciousness unheard of with today's cramped, hectic air travel. On the 804-foot *Hindenburg*, the seventy-two passengers were served by a crew of fifty. Cabins, nestled in the lower interior of the sausage, were heated and equipped with hot and cold running water. A menu lists meals such as "boneless squab pigeon with *foie gras*," served at linen-covered tables set with fresh flowers. Bread and pastries were baked fresh daily. Passengers could make telephone calls to Europe and America. There was a reading room, a writing room, a bar, and a lounge with a grand piano from which concerts were broadcast to radio stations in America. (The piano was made from aluminum, and weighed only 397 pounds.) There was even a special smoking room, pressurized to keep out any leaking hydrogen. The lighters there were chained down; the passengers' own were confiscated for duration of the voyage. Since the *Hindenburg* usually cruised at about 800 feet, a popular pastime was strolling the two 46-foot-long promenade decks, looking at the ground or ocean below through large, plexiglass windows.

There was more to the magic of the airship than its luxury. It's one of those few feats of engineering that stirs the soul, like a full-rigged sailing ship or a suspension bridge. Dr. Hugo Eckener, the great pilot and chairman of the Zeppelin company, understood its almost mystical appeal. He described the airship as "a fabulous silvery fish, floating quietly in the ocean of air and captivating the eye just like a fantastic, exotic fish seen in an aquarium. And this fairy-like apparition, which seemed to melt into the silvery-blue background of sky, when it appeared far away, lighted by the sun, seemed to be coming from another world and to be returning there like a dream." After leaving the Lakehurst, N.J., landing field, Zeppelins would fly low over Manhattan, skimming just 160 feet above the Woolworth and Singer buildings (at the time there were no regulations on flight heights). They made an unearthly drone, from the sound of their engines reverberating off the overhanging envelope. Traffic would halt and work cease while the crowds stared awestruck as the airships, big as ocean liners, passed overhead. The Germans gave it a term—"Zeppelin Fever."

The great age of airship travel ended on May 6, 1937, with the *Hindenburg* disaster at Lakehurst. The 36 who lost their lives out of the 93 aboard were the first casualties of a commercial airship accident. Over the years, the German Zeppelins had safely flown more than 32,000 passengers over 1,000,000 miles, but the searing image of the burning *Hindenburg* , with newsman Herb Morrison sobbing "Oh, the humanity!" into his mike, was hard to overcome, and seems to serve as a vaccine against any widespread resurgence of Zeppelin fever.

Actually, airship travel was problematic at the best of times. The Germans were the only ones who really had the knack of it, and their pilots flew more by instinct and daring than by standardized procedures. Hugo Eckener would fly directly at a mountain and assure his nervous crew, "Don't worry, the moving air mass we're in will carry us right over it." Wouldn't that sound great on a black-box flight recording? The ships were particularly vulnerable to wind shears, which could tear a dirigible to pieces. The British halted their dirigible program after the *R-101* disaster, the Americans after the wrecks of the U.S. Navy's *Shenandoah*, *Akron*, and *Macon*.

Still, there are advantages of lighter-than-air travel that make engineers and investors continually reconsider the dirigible. Air resistance to its huge bulk puts a practical upper limit on airship speed of about 120 mph—slower than a plane, but much faster than a boat. Unlike a plane, it requires no airport, and needs not land to take on or unload cargo, and unlike a boat it can travel inland. Though expensive to build, it is cheap to operate. The *Hindenburg* weighed 240 tons, but when afloat in calm

air could be pushed by a child. Loaded with 70 passengers and 13 tons of freight, it required only $500 worth of cheap diesel fuel to cross the Atlantic. Since it doesn't consume fuel to stay in the air, the dirigible can remain aloft for extraordinary periods—on one occasion, arriving in Brazil after a 5,942 mile trip to find a mini-revolution in progress, the *Graf Zeppelin* stood out to sea for three days until order was restored.

There have been so many proposals to reintroduce variations of the dirigible that they could account for the expression, "a trial balloon." Many have been aimed at freight hauling. There was the Megalifter, a winged dolphin powered by jet engines. There was the Cyclo-Crane, built by the AeroLift company. There was the Aereon III, or "trigible," a three-hulled dirigible in which over $100,000 was invested in 1962. A major effort went into the Heli-Stat, a blimp connected to four tailless helicopters mounted on a frame, intended to be used to remove timber from cutting areas without the need to put in logging roads. The Forest Service supported development to the tune of $40 million, earning it one of Senator Proxmire's Golden Fleece awards for wasting the taxpayer's money. In 1986, the helium-buoyed vessel crashed and burned while being tested. The sight of its demise was Lakehurst, N.J., and perhaps sensing the hand of fate, no further funds were invested in the project.

In the early sixties, Boston University aeronautical engineer Francis Morse proposed the Nuclear Airship, a 980-foot-long dirigible powered by a nuclear powerplant. It would travel at about 100 mph, slightly over the *Hindenburg's* top speed of 84 mph, and would cross the Atlantic in less than two days. Its 400 passengers would enjoy luxurious accommodations; staterooms with private baths, a movie theater, even a skyroom cocktail lounge atop the dirigible, reachable by elevator. Since it would not require refueling it could stay aloft indefinitely, its passengers arriving and disembarking by shuttle plane. An all-cargo version would transport 150 cars across the ocean at about $140 each. The plan received considerable attention, including enthusiastic coverage in *Esquire,* complete with artist's renditions of the sumptuous possibilities. At the time, engineers had been looking at the possibility of nuclear-powered airplanes. Since a reactor big enough to power a Boeing 707 would require 225,000 lbs. of radiation shielding, the idea was dismissed as impractical. However, a dirigible requires only 6,000 hp to the 707's 40,000, so its powerplant and shielding would be considerably lighter, and comfortably within the airship's 300,000 pound lifting capacity. It was also felt that any crash of the Nuclear Airship would be slow and gentle, and would reduce the possibility that radioactive material would be spewed far and wide. Reassurances aside, most of us are grateful that among our other worries we do not have Nuclear Airships cruising around overhead.

SOURCES

Many of the topics in this book were researched through contemporary articles in *Time, Life, Newsweek, U.S. News and World Report, Business Week, Esquire, People Weekly, New Yorker, The Wall Street Journal* and *The New York Times*. A number of primary sources were also interviewed. Books that provided material include:

Addams, Charles. *Dear Dead Days.* G.P. Putnam's Sons, 1959.

Andrews, Bart. *The Worst TV Shows—Ever: Those TV Turkeys We Will Never Forget...(No Matter How Hard We Try).* Dutton, 1980.

Burroughs, Bryan and Helyar, John. *Barbarians At the Gate, The Fall of RJR Nabisco.* Harper & Row, 1990.

Feinberg, Rick. *Peculiar Patents.* A Citadel Press Book, Carol Publishing Group, 1994.

Felton, Bruce and Fowler, Mark. *The Best, Worst & Most Unusual.* Galahad Books, 1994.

Gardner, Martin. *Fads & Fallacies in the Name of Science.* New American Library, 1986.

Gilbert, James. *The World's Worst Aircraft.* St. Martin's Press, 1975.

Gill, Brendan, *Many Masks, A Life of Frank Lloyd Wright.* Putnam, 1987.

Goldberg, Lee. *Unsold T.V. Pilots.* A Citadel Press Book, Carol Publishing Group, 1991.

Goldberg, M. Hirsh. *The Blunder Book.* Morrow, 1984.

Guterman, Jimmy and O'Donnell, Owen. *The Worst Rock-And-Roll Records of All Time: A Fan's Guide to the Stuff You Love to Hate.* Carol Publishing Group, 1991.

Hatch, Alden. *Buckminster Fuller—At Home in the Universe.* Crown, 1974.

Hendon, Donald. *Classic Failures in Product Marketing.* Quorum Books, 1989.

Hoffman, Frank and Bailey, William. *Arts & Entertainment Fads.* The Haworth Press, 1990.

Hoffman, Frank and Bailey, William. *Sports & Recreation Fads.* The Haworth Press, 1991.

Hoffman, Frank and Bailey, William. *Mind & Society Fads.* The Haworth Press, 1992.

Hoffman, Frank and Bailey, William. *Fashion & Merchandising Fads.* The Haworth Press, 1994.

Jacobs, Timothy. *Lemons: The World's Worst Cars.* Barnes & Noble, Inc., 1994.

Javna, John and Gordon. *60s!* St. Martin's Press, 1982.

Josephson, Matthew. *Edison.* McGraw, Hill, 1959.

Lauber, John. *The Inventions of Mark Twain*. Hill & Wang—a division of Farrar, Straus & Giroux, 1990.

Lorant, Stefan. *The Life and Times of Theodore Roosevelt*. Doubleday & Co., Inc., 1959.

Lord, Athena V. *Pilot for Spaceship Earth: R. Buckminster Fuller*. MacMillan Publishing Co., Inc., 1978.

Mason, Roy. *Xanadu: The Computerized Home of Tomorrow and How It Can Be Yours Today!* Acropolis Books, 1983.

Medved, Harry and Michael. *The Hollywood Hall of Shame: The Most Expensive Flops in Movie History*. Perigree Books, 1984.

Michell, John. *Eccentric Lives and Peculiar Notions*. New York. Harcourt Brace Jovanovich, 1984.

Murphy, Jim. *Weird & Wacky Inventions*. New York. Crown Publishers, Inc., 1978.

Oliver, Thomas. *The Real Coke, The Real Story*. Random House, 1986.

Onosko, Tim. *Wasn't the Future Wonderful?* Dutton, 1979.

Panati, Charles. *Panati's Parade of Fads, Follies and Manias: The Origins of Our Most Cherished Obsessions*. Harper Perennial, 1991.

Pile, Stephen. *The Incomplete Book of Failures: The Official Handbook of the Not-Terribly-Good Club of Great Britain*. Dutton, 1979.

Reader's Digest. *Strange Stories, Amazing Facts*. The Reader's Digest Association, 1976.

Reader's Digest. *Discovering America's Past*. The Reader's Digest Association, 1993.

Re/Search #14. *Incredibly Strange Music*. Re/Search Publications, 1993.

Ricks, David. *Big Business Blunders*. Dow Jones-Irwin, 1991.

Rooney, Mickey. *Life Is Too Short*. Villard Books, 1991.

Sann, Paul. *Fads, Follies and Delusions of the American People*. Bonanza Books, 1967.

Skolnick, Peter. *Fads: America's Crazes, Fevers and Fancies from the 1890s to the 1970s*. Crowell, 1978.

Steinberg, Neil. *Complete & Utter Failure*. New York. Doubleday, 1994.

Stern, Jane and Michael. *Sixties People*. Knopf, 1990.

Stern, Sydney, and Schoenhaus, Ted. *Toyland: The High-Stakes Game of the Toy Industry*. Chicago. Contemporary Books, 1990.

Wall, John Frazier. *Andrew Carnegie*. Oxford University Press, 1970.

Wallechinsky, David; Wallace, Irving; and Wallace, Amy. *Book of Lists*. Cassell, 1977.

Yenne, Bill. *The World's Worst Aircraft*. Greenwich. Dorset Press, 1993.

Images from the book are courtesy Movie Still Archives, patents and public domain, catalogs and photos courtesy of individual organizations, and the New Coke picture courtesy UPI/BETTMAN. Additional illustrations were generously supplied by Paul Kirchner.

Rhino Records is known primarily for its quality reissues of the great music of the past...but Rhino also has an affinity for the flop. Our recent venture into the book world was delightfully inaugurated by *The Best of The World's Worst* by Stan Lee. We also invite you to happily endure such classic films as Ed Wood's *Plan 9 From Outer Space* or *The Brain That Wouldn't Die* on video—or the marginal magnificence of albums like *Golden Throats 3: Sweethearts of Rodeo Drive*, where celebrities such as Leonard Nimoy, Goldie Hawn and Buddy Ebsen massacre songs by Johnny Cash, Bob Dylan and Hank Williams, or *Dead Parrot Society*, a best of British comedy sampler, on CD or cassette.

To get a Rhino catalogue, call (800) 432-0020.